Time Manage[r]
for Lawyers
Making Every
Six Minutes Count

EDITED BY ALEX DAVIES
WITH A FOREWORD BY CATRIN MILLS

Commissioning editor
Alex Davies

Managing director
Sian O'Neill

Time Management for Lawyers: Making Every Six Minutes Count
is published by

Globe Law and Business Ltd
3 Mylor Close
Horsell
Woking
Surrey GU21 4DD
United Kingdom
Tel: +44 20 3745 4770
www.globelawandbusiness.com

Time Management for Lawyers: Making Every Six Minutes Count

ISBN 978-1-83723-134-8
EPUB ISBN 978-1-83723-135-5
Adobe PDF ISBN 978-1-83723-136-2

GPSR Compliance: EU Authorised Representative: Easy Access System Europe - Mustamäe tee 50, 10621 Tallinn, Estonia, gpsr.requests@easproject.com

Contents

Executive summary

Time Management for Lawyers: Making Every Six Minutes Count is a comprehensive guide designed to help legal professionals take control of their time and enhance both productivity and wellbeing. In a fast-paced and high-pressure profession, time management is the key to thriving – not just surviving. This book explores practical strategies for managing overwhelming caseloads, maintaining a healthy work–life balance, and preventing burnout. It covers the latest technological influences, including how AI is reshaping how lawyers manage time and tasks, while also addressing the mental and emotional challenges of working in law.

From optimizing focus to managing client demands and avoiding distractions, this book helps lawyers achieve peak performance while still leaving room for creativity, innovation, and personal wellbeing. With expert advice on delegation, prioritization and setting clear goals, *Time Management for Lawyers: Making Every Six Minutes Count* equips you with the tools to reclaim your time and thrive in your legal career.

The book opens with a foreword by Catrin Mills, a solicitor with over 25 years' experience, who explores how the issue of time poverty for lawyers isn't going away. Catrin outlines the issues and gives an overview of what is to come in the book.

Chapter one, by Todd Hutchison, then looks at tools and techniques lawyers can use to schedule and prioritize their time, taking into account task importance, with consideration to their unique behavioral styles, energy levels, and the ways in which they best work.

This is followed by chapter two on prioritization, and how to focus on what matters the most. David Skinner and Karen Dunn Skinner explore the real cost of doing it all, contrasting this approach with the high-value work only you can do. They also explore the concept of delegation, offering tools and strategies to find ways to reclaim your time and reimagine your practice.

In chapter three, Joanna Gaudoin looks at how you can make time for business development – that essential but often overlooked aspect of work that gets lost in the day-to-day.

Joanna explores the key building blocks you need to make time for, and how to build business development into your working day. In chapter four, Jean-Baptiste Lebelle and Alice Boullier de Branche of A&O Shearman look at work–life balance and wellbeing, and how to protect your health and energy.

Wellbeing and effective time management stand at the core of long-term performance and satisfaction in business law. Legal professionals face distinctive challenges, such as the constant pressure to be available and the frequent merging of work and personal life due to urgent client needs. Addressing these challenges is vital not only for individual lawyers but also for the overall health of the profession. Chapter four rethinks work–life balance as a dynamic equilibrium, looking at its consequences and benefits from a scientific standpoint. The authors then look at strategies for sustainable practice, by both the individual and the organization, recognizing that a shared commitment to a healthy work environment is essential for the future of business law. The chapter concludes with tips on how lawyers can thrive through sustainable time management. By leveraging technology, prioritizing wellbeing, and fostering a supportive culture, lawyers can reclaim their time, enhance performance, and build fulfilling, sustainable careers.

In chapter five, Nikki Alderson explores how the COVID-19 pandemic forced a long-overdue transformation in the legal profession – away from rigid presenteeism and towards more flexible, remote-first models of working. Drawing on first-hand client experience and industry trends, she examines whether working from home has improved or undermined productivity, inclusion, and wellbeing. The chapter offers a balanced perspective on the pros and cons of remote legal work, alongside concrete, practical strategies for leaders, individuals, and teams to cultivate focus, connection, and sustainable success in a post-pandemic world.

AI is actively changing time management in legal practice today – not in some distant future. It is not replacing lawyers, but helping them reclaim time and reduce their admin burden. Chapter six by Sarah Murphy gives concrete examples of how AI can streamline task management, reduce context switching, and improve client responsiveness. Using Clio Duo as a case study, Sarah encourages lawyers to reflect on their current workflows and consider trialing AI tools to improve productivity.

In chapter seven, Gary Miles explores the prevailing culture of busyness, and how to break free from constant overload. The chapter looks at why lawyers are more stressed and overwhelmed than ever and how to combat the culture of busyness in order to create time for strategic thinking.

Chapter eight by Mila Trezza explores the "always-on" mindset and its underlying causes, including a culture of busyness and constant responsiveness, years of training to develop accuracy, pressure to double- and triple-check work, a drive to be "on top of things", under-resourced teams, and a desire to excel. Over time, difficulty switching off can become an ingrained habit, spiraling into an "always-on" mindset that ultimately undermines the very productivity we aim to achieve. Mila's chapter provides a foundation for an intentional shift towards a more sustainable way of working – one that enables us to take control of our time and priorities. It also offers practical strategies for setting realistic boundaries with clients and colleagues, and shows how effective communication can help us ensure these boundaries stay in place while delivering to client expectations.

In the high-stakes world of legal practice, time is precious – but attention is priceless. Lawyers are trained to manage calendars, juggle deadlines, and prioritize caseloads. But what if the real key to productivity isn't in your planner, but in your brain? Chapter nine by Anna Marra takes you inside the science of neuroproductivity – the art of aligning your work habits with how your brain functions. Rather than pushing harder and longer, you'll discover how to work smarter by leveraging the natural rhythms of attention, decision-making, memory, and mental energy. With practical strategies grounded in neuroscience, this chapter will help you reclaim control – not just of your schedule, but of your mind. For lawyers who want to thrive, not just survive, neuroproductivity offers a new lens for time management, one that starts from the inside out.

Chapter ten then looks at how to make space for creativity – a path to well-being and peak performance that Karen Dunn Skinner believes is essential. Karen acknowledges the high-stress, high-performance expectations in law and introduces the idea that creativity – often dismissed or ignored in legal culture – is not a distraction but a powerful productivity tool that supports better service delivery and improved quality of life for lawyers. Creative activities (artistic and otherwise) reduce stress, replenish mental energy, and can improve decision-making and client service. Time spent on creative pursuits, Karen argues, is not wasted – it fuels higher performance at work.

Todd Hutchison returns in chapter 11 to look at career planning and strategic time management. Carving out time for long-term career goals and growth is essential he maintains, as well as stepping back from daily tasks to focus on your professional trajectory.

Rachel Brushfield then continues this theme in chapter 12, exploring how lawyers can master time for a successful legal career. She examines the importance of taking time to plan your career and make it future proof, sharing examples of how to make time to plan your career with a busy life and workload, and strategic tools and frameworks that you can apply to your own career now and in the future.

Rachel explores the technique of career scenario planning and how this can help you to look at different career options and mitigate risk. The role of environment as a useful way of creating focus for career planning is analyzed, ring-fencing space as well as time to focus on your future career. The emergence of Artificial Intelligence (AI) and how it can be useful for expedient career planning is also analyzed.

About the authors

Nikki Alderson is an international talent retention and women's leadership specialist, TEDx and keynote speaker, coach, bestselling author of *Raising the Bar: Empowering female lawyers through coaching*, and former criminal barrister with 19 years' experience. Nikki supports law firms, barristers' Chambers, and other legal organizations to attract, retain, and elevate female talent and empowers female lawyers and other professionals to achieve career ambitions. Nikki specializes in three areas – women's leadership, enhanced career break return and new working parent support, and workplace resilience, confidence, and wellbeing. Although Nikki's work focuses predominantly on one-to-one coaching within the workplace, she also delivers motivational keynote speeches and bespoke workshops, seminars and webinars on a variety of topics, such as *Breaking Barriers to being your Best, Return and Rise, Finding Time to Have it All*, and *Workplace Wellbeing*.

Alice Boullier de Branche is senior HR manager in the Paris HR team at A&O Shearman. She graduated from business school (ESSEC Global BBA) and has a master's degree in Sociology (Paris VII). Alice has been working on HR matters at A&O Shearman for over ten years. She joined A&O to work on training and development, then later specialized in providing human resources support to the fee earners population. She is especially engaged in areas such as performance evaluation, compensation strategies, recruitment, retention, and talent development, as well as wellbeing, diversity, and inclusion initiatives. Alice has contributed to a book produced for the International Bar Association by Globe Law & Business, *Talent in the Legal Profession*.

Rachel Brushfield is "The Talent Liberator"™®, and founder of EnergiseLegal, established in 1996. An experienced career strategist and coach with a marketing and brand strategy career heritage, Rachel helps mid-career lawyers overcome actual and perceived blocks and create an uplifting career breakthrough at major career crossroads. Women lawyers, portfolio careers, personal branding, and consultant lawyers are specialisms. Content creation projects include career webinars for the Law Society and D+I content for LexisNexis. Rachel is a published author in multiple topics including marketing, career management, professional development, and talent management. A seasoned events professional, Rachel has done multiple events for women lawyer networks including the Law Society UK, the Law Society Northern Ireland, Society of English and American Lawyers (SEAL), American Women Lawyers in London (AWLL), and Women in the Law (WITL).

Karen Dunn Skinner coaches legal professionals around the world to be as great at running their businesses as they are at practicing law. She believes lawyers can have it all – a thriving practice and a life they love. After more than 20 years as a lawyer, she co-founded Gimbal Consulting with her partner, David. Karen is a pioneer in legal process improvement, the author of *The Power Zone Playbook for Lawyers*, and a sought-after speaker and consultant. She's a global advisor to the International Institute of Legal Project Management and a fellow of the College of Law Practice Management. Karen lives in Montreal, where she and David have raised two children and built a fulfilling life they love. In the last few years, she's rediscovered painting and finds tremendous inspiration when she's hiking and skiing at Tremblant or paddling her kayak on the St Lawrence River. Her art has given her a whole new understanding of the relationship between creativity, productivity, and happiness.

Joanna Gaudoin helps professional services firms and their people take a structured and skilled approach to business development. Many professionals find winning and retaining challenging, yet it's a core part of their role. Joanna helps individuals and firms build clarity, confidence, and capability to develop and retain valuable client relationships. Through her company, ClientWise, Joanna works to reduce over-reliance on a few individuals bringing in work and supports a more consistent, embedded approach to growth. Her work spans consultancy, facilitation, and training through firm-wide programs, targeted workshops, and individual coaching. Her proven framework, The 5 Ps of Business Development©, underpins all her work. Joanna has 14+ years of experience with law firms, accountants, banks, and other professional services. She previously worked in brand marketing and consultancy. She's an experienced and engaging speaker and author of *Getting On: Making work work*, and co-author of two other Globe Law and

Business titles, *Business Development for Women Lawyers* and *Essential Reads for the Modern Lawyer.*

Dr Todd Hutchison is an international bestselling author, and listed in the *Who's Who of Business in Australia.* He is the global chairman of the International Institute of Legal Project Management (IILPM), which has legal practitioner graduates in 65 countries. He is a consultant with commercial law firm Balfour Meagher, an adjunct associate professor (Business and Law) at Edith Cowan University, and teaches business law, contract law, and project management in an MBA program. His fascination with high performance led to his studies in behavioral science and he has personally led projects in over 260 organizations across 21 countries. He completed a doctorate in forensics and legal project management, and works as a digital forensic expert witness in Supreme Court cases across Australia, specializing in homicide and major crime matters.

Jean-Baptiste Lebelle is the HR director of A&O Shearman's Paris office. He holds a law degree from Paris II Assas and graduated from Sciences Po Paris. Jean-Baptiste has taught at the Sorbonne and HEC on recruitment, retention, and career management in law firms. He has over 25 years of HR experience in the consulting sector and is especially engaged in topics related to compensation policies, recruitment, talent retention, inclusion, and well-being applied to law firms. He switched from headhunting for law firms to HR, becoming PWC Legal's HR director for Paris before A&O. Jean-Baptiste Lebelle has contributed to several books produced for the International Bar Association by Globe Law & Business.

Anna Marra is an Italian consultant and trainer, based in Spain, specializing in strategic and operational legal project management for law firms and corporate legal departments. She graduated in Law from the University of Milan, has been a member of the Varese Bar Association since 2004, and holds a Master's degree in International Affairs from the Institute for International Political Studies (ISPI) in Milan. She served as the executive director of Transparency International Italy, contributing to educational and legislative initiatives on ethics and anti-corruption. Since 2006, she has focused on legal project management, merging her legal expertise with project methodologies to introduce innovative approaches in legal matter management, becoming an international reference in this field. Anna is deputy chair of the International Institute of Legal Project Management (IILPM) and an advisor for the Global LegalTech Hub. She has authored books such as *Legal Project Management: Techniques to Innovate in the Legal Market* (2012) and *LPM Bites – Purpose-Driven Management: A Humanistic Approach to Legal Project Management* (2025). As the director of various international open and on-demand courses on legal project management and legal productivity, she founded the LPMFocused Hub in 2023 for legal professionals interested in new work frameworks, productivity, efficiency, and sustainability in legal practice.

Gary Miles, a seasoned law practitioner for over four decades, has dedicated his career to litigation and, more recently, family law. As the managing member of Huesman, Jones, and Miles in Maryland for over three decades, his diverse experience includes being a trial lawyer, managing partner, author, leader, podcaster, coach, and entrepreneur. His true passion lies in helping lawyers solve their problems and guiding them toward liberation from the hurdles that hold them back. Having experienced the pressures inherent in the legal profession, Gary is deeply committed to his clients' success and fulfilment. He equips them with practical tools to overcome the obstacles they face, enabling them to achieve the success and freedom they aspire to in their law practices. Gary's influence extends beyond the courtroom. He hosts a popular, highly-rated podcast, The Free Lawyer, with two weekly episodes, and is the author of the insightful book *Breaking Free*. These platforms allow him to share his knowledge and experience with a broader audience.

Catrin Mills has over 25 years' experience as a practicing solicitor specializing in employment law. Catrin trained with a City firm before pursuing her career outside London to become a partner in Hertford. Catrin has recently returned to private practice having spent a period in-house with a leading independent school where she became chief operating officer. Catrin has always had a keen interest in people management and especially how individual productivity and staff engagement contribute to the success of an organization. She now advises both employers and employees on all aspects of employment law, and particularly enjoys supporting employer clients with people strategy.

Sarah Murphy is the general manager of Clio International, overseeing EMEA, APAC, and Canada for Clio, the global leader in legal technology. With a strong emphasis on innovation, she leads and inspires her teams, ensuring Clio remains at the forefront of transforming the legal experience across these diverse regions. Sarah's extensive career spans various industries, including finance, insurance, telecommunications, and legal technology. This diverse expertise enables her to empower legal professionals of all backgrounds to overcome the challenges of running successful law firms. Driven by her passion for building and scaling high-growth teams, Sarah combines a commitment to innovation with a focus on customer success and exploring new markets where Clio can make a significant impact. As the driving force behind Clio's expansion across EMEA, APAC and beyond, Sarah unlocks untapped opportunities and steers Clio towards continued success. Under her leadership, Clio consistently sets new standards of excellence and innovation throughout the region.

David Skinner believes lawyers can have it all – a thriving practice and a life they love. The co-founder of Gimbal Consulting and the LeanLegal® Academy, he's a Lean Six Sigma expert and lawyer with decades of experience in private practice and in-house in Canada, Europe, and the UK. David combines his profound knowledge of the practice with the perspective he gained as a client, to help lawyers build profitable and productive practices. David is a sought-after thought leader and consultant. He's the co-author of *The Power Zone Playbook for Lawyers* and a global advisor to the International Institute of Legal Project Management. David has facilitated process improvement projects across North America and taught Gimbal's proven LeanLegal® approach to thousands of legal professionals. David was a member of the bars of Quebec, Massachusetts, and New York for over 30 years. He splits his time between Montreal and Mont-Tremblant and dedicates hundreds of hours a year to volunteering as a ski patroller and rescue technician.

Mila Trezza is a former general counsel and vice president for a Fortune Global 500 energy company. With over 20 years of international experience as a lawyer, she is now an award-winning executive coach. Through her coaching, Mila partners with legal leaders and organizations worldwide – including global corporations, top-tier law firms, and leading in-house teams – to reframe challenges, strengthen leadership, and build the confidence needed to create meaningful impact and sustainable growth. Her contributions to the legal profession have been recognized with numerous awards, including a Lifetime Achievement Award (In-House) from ALM | Women, Influence & Power in Law UK.

Foreword

When the first edition of this book was published, social media was in its infancy and whilst commentators had for some time been warning of the existential threat of AI, technology had not yet solved a lawyer's eternal problem – how to find more time in every day.

We might have anticipated that, by now, technological advancements would have helped us to master the competing pressures that are an inevitable part of a lawyer's daily experience. We might have expected that by 2025 we would be awash with time-saving applications or that with novel business structures and new charging models we might have left behind the billable hour entirely.

But how much has really changed? The world, and the way lawyers work, might have altered dramatically, but the demands on lawyers are arguably more intense than ever.

The pressure to be always available, meeting financial targets under cost scrutiny, and making time for business development in a crowded market-place, can leave little time to fit in other essentials like personal development and wellbeing. The communication channels open to clients and colleagues have multiplied with the addition of online meetings and chat messaging, meaning that we are constantly reachable. Time management is still a real challenge for lawyers in our fast-paced "always-on" culture.

This book starts with a fresh look at prioritization and task management and offers some useful advice for effective scheduling. It emphasizes the disadvantages of attempting to plan when in a state of chronic stress or overwhelm and provides practical tips on how to tap into our logical mind for better decision-making. It introduces us to behavioral styles and encourages us to think about aligning tasks with our natural talents to achieve a state of high productivity and fulfilment, or "flow".

The book goes on to consider the importance of work–life balance and wellbeing and how, as a result of the pandemic, the profession was reluctantly forced to adopt flexible working almost overnight. It is perhaps ironic that a profession in which individuals (at least those of us in private practice) must routinely record and justify how they allocate their daily hours was so suspicious of allowing lawyers to work autonomously, but many would argue that concentrated time, free from interruptions, has led to increased productivity. Whether working from home is here to stay is a matter of debate, but a balance needs to be struck with team communication, support for more junior lawyers, and ensuring that the blurring of the line between home and work does not lead to burnout.

The contributors then go on to offer helpful strategies to combat overload, such as how to set boundaries and then stick to them. We are also reminded of the need for leaders to model good work–life balance, and how taking care of our own wellbeing enables us to serve our clients better.

Delegation is, we know, key to effective time management, and now we can delegate tasks to the world of AI. Lawyers are being encouraged to embrace productivity-enhancing tools and the book provides useful examples of how technology can be used to relieve the administrative burden on lawyers, or to ease data-heavy tasks. Lawyers are now routinely adopting AI not just to automate administrative processes, but to "do the leg work" – from creating initial drafts or analyzing lengthy contracts to producing attendance notes or summarizing legal research, and that is surely the tip of the iceberg.

The science of "neuroproductivity" explains the role of the brain's different rhythms for the purpose of different types of tasks, such as critical thinking and problem solving. It highlights the effect of technology and interruptions on how the brain works and, importantly, how stress affects decision-making. We learn how accessing these rhythms can enhance productivity and optimize focus to avoid chronic stress. On the topic of a healthy mind, we're also encouraged to make time for creative activities to offset cognitive overload and to allow our subconscious to bring us new levels of insight.

Finally, we are reminded of the importance of seeing the bigger picture – our day-to-day work should lead us towards our career goals. This book provides helpful advice on how to think strategically about our careers and ambitions. Using behavioral profiling we learn how understanding and channeling our natural abilities brings not just productivity but professional fulfilment.

This book is a long-awaited update to the previous edition, providing practical, evidence-based strategies to help lawyers take back control. Applicable to legal professionals at every stage of their career, whether you're in private practice, in-house, self-employed, or enjoying a portfolio career, it is an essential companion for any lawyer who wants to create a successful – and sustainable – working life.

Catrin Mills

Chapter 1:
A work day unique to you – understanding your own working rhythms

By Dr Todd Hutchison, global chair, International Institute of Legal Project Management

"The key is not to prioritize what's on your schedule, but to schedule your priorities."
Stephen R. Covey

Effective prioritization is about operating from a logical mind state to enable precision decision-making that determines the correct ordering of tasks to bring the best results. These decisions need to be supported by high performance to get the key priority tasks accomplished in the shortest amount of time, considering both their urgency and importance. Productivity also benefits from maximizing the use of your behavioral style and energy for what you should progress, compared to what you should be delegating to someone else who may be more effective at the task.

Although the whole process is centered on the construct of "time", time management in itself is a fallacy, as time is fixed. Rather, it is more about "schedule management", which is largely about prioritizing tasks and determining when the best time is to work on each item to achieve higher productivity.

A personal "action list" is a common term for any tool that lists pending work to be analyzed and prioritized (although it can be used in other contexts for group work, such as for project teams), yet does not assure higher productivity, but rather defines the order to progress work. Beyond prioritizing tasks, we will explore a holistic process that leads to getting the highest quantity of the most relevant work done. It involves our thinking, how we order tasks that are most relevant to be done as a priority, getting clarity to who does the work, and how we can get the most tasks done in the shortest amount of time.

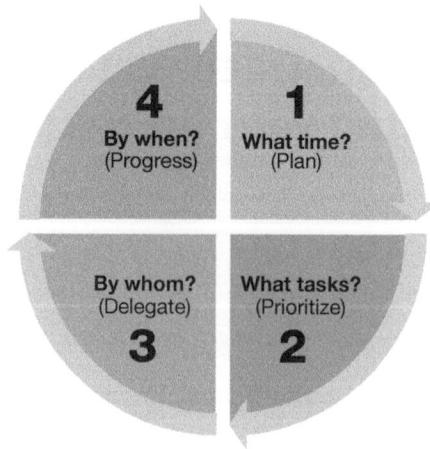

Figure 1: Questions to ask when planning work.

Step 1: Plan – effective planning in the right mental state

Effective prioritization relies heavily on using logical cognitive processes that enable reasoning in a structured and analytical way. Emotions, such as being in a state of overwhelm, can directly affect your ability to think clearly and logically. Your mind can get highjacked by your emotions. This is where any form of planning becomes a hard task.

The human brain operates with two different states – logical and emotional. Although this is a simplification to the complexities of the brain, the prefrontal cortex is known to drive logical thought, whilst the limbic system, especially the amygdala, drives emotions that influence thought. It is the emotional system that triggers first to new situations like threats. Therefore, in an emotional state, it is difficult to be effective at critically examining tasks in a comparative manner to determine their best order to progress.

Modern leadership education emphasizes the need for "emotional intelligence", which is simply a phrase for maintaining your logical state, where it can evaluate and override emotional impulses. The logical system, often referred to as the "logical brain" or "thinking brain" allows for self-control, reasoning, planning, decision-making, and problem solving. This is the system where prioritization is enabled to analyze and compare tasks to determine their relative importance, urgency, and value to best determine an order to progress.

When the emotional system is engaged, often referred to as the "emotional brain" or "feeling brain", it triggers emotive and reactive actions, like the flight, fight, or freeze response. It is also the key driver of memory formulation, where the brain uses the level of emotion to determine what is important to store, hence why you remember the best and worst times of your life. It places you in a connected state, whereas logic operates more like an objective thinker.

The state of overwhelm inhibits the ability to schedule tasks, where your logical brain is switched off, and you don't know what to do next, and where procrastination becomes most dominating. The process to follow to resolve feeling overwhelmed is to say to yourself, *"What is the very next thing?"* and just do that. Then pick the very next thing, and just do that, and finally in repeating the same process, pick the very next thing, and just do that. After three focused tasks, you should have shifted from the emotional brain controlling you to the logical brain. You should now be out of the overwhelm state. This is an example of how extreme emotions can be controlled.

Planning your tasks therefore requires you to be in a logical state. The first step is to identify the best time for you to prioritize your tasks. Some people choose to do it at the start of their day, as generally they have not been interrupted by the busyness it will bring, whilst others like to do it at the end of the day to consolidate where they got to, and to reprioritize what still has to be done. Confirming when you will do your prioritization and then making it part of your everyday routine will provide better results.

Step 2: Prioritize – ordering the action list tasks
When you first start the process of making an action list, you have to brainstorm the outstanding tasks that need to be progressed. Once you have the list, it is simply a process of maintaining the list by adding new tasks, deleting completed tasks, and sometimes removing unnecessary tasks. Having the list handy helps to document any new initiative that you become aware of or comes into your consciousness.

Having an action list also contributes to stress management. You may have noticed that on leaving the office, your mind starts making you consciously aware of tasks you may have forgotten to do, such as send an email, speak to someone, follow up on something, or make a call. The mind will keep reminding you, until you have a system that allows you to get it out of your head and on to a list. The brain will let it go if it thinks you now have it under control. This works the same when sleeping, where people have a pen and paper next to the bed, to write down their interrupting thoughts about an outstanding or forgotten task that is keeping them awake. When it is only in your head, the brain likes to look at a single item from multiple angles, so that you feel there are many tasks to deal with, which can actually lead to more stress.

By having an action list, you will free up your thinking, at which point a prioritization process will enable you to just focus on the next task. It forces the logical brain back into control.

Given there is no single tool or method to prioritize, you have to find a system that works for you. Whilst the use of technology and the availability of mobile smart phones and watches allows you to immediately edit your task list, some people still prefer writing an action list on paper. The action of ticking off a completed task gives a release of dopamine, which is a motivational and reward neurochemical that gives you a feeling of pleasure, as well as boosting serotonin that helps stabilize your mind, and other feel-good endorphins. Ticking off a task in writing likely intensifies the experience, and therefore is a stronger emotional event than simply pressing a button on an app.

From a process perspective, once you are operating in a logical state and you have your list of tasks, it then comes down to allocating the right tasks in the best order to progress them. It may not be your preferred order, as urgent tasks that arise may not be important to you, but might be time-sensitive and often have consequences if not completed.

Whilst an urgent task requires immediate action and focus, it can bring psychological pressure. When broken down, urgent tasks reflect what is happening in your life today, and stem from deadlines, demands, and (often) other people's priorities. In fact, poor planning and inefficient work habits can cause tasks to become urgent, as they are not otherwise getting done in a timely fashion, when time simply runs out.

Much has been written about the criticality of analyzing both urgent and important tasks. It is the important tasks that are generally significant to your future and what can shift and shape your life. For example, a lawyer may want to complete a Master of Laws that could be beneficial for their career enhancement, but they might not be able to find the time to enroll and progress it. Arguably, this is not a time issue – it is a priority and scheduling issue.

This is where delegation comes into play. Although an urgent task requires an immediate response due to a real or perceived crisis or critical deadline, it does not mean that you personally have to do it – rather the fact that it just needs to get done by someone. Before we delegate though, we need to prioritize which tasks need to be progressed in what order, and then consider who is best placed to do it based on skill and availability.

There are many methods and tools to prioritize tasks. Below we look at some different models.

Method 1 – Urgency driven approach

The fastest method for prioritizing tasks is to have four columns on a spreadsheet (see Figure 1):

1. *Task description* – where column 1 represents each task on the list.
2. *Priority* – where in column 2 you allocate a "1" (or some other mark) to all the urgent tasks, or allocate a "1" to all the tasks that are both urgent and important. If any new tasks come up between your core planning time, you keep adding them to the list, with particular interest in those that get a "1" priority rating that could cause a reorganization of the priority of those already ordered.

    For a more in-depth variation, you could extend the rankings to specific periods of time, such as:

    1 – must be done today;

    2 – must be done by tomorrow;

    3 – must be done over a three- to four-day period;

    4 – should be progressed within a week;

    5 – should be progressed this month; and

    6 – does not need to be scheduled.

3. *Order [to progress]* – where in column 3 you allocate a sequential number (or letter) for those tasks set to a "1" in column 2. This now creates the absolute order you will undertake the tasks in – with consideration to their urgency, or urgency and importance.

    This means you need to get into the habit of following that order, rather than jumping to the fun or easy ones. Staying disciplined allows you to progress with the prioritization order you set in your logical state.

    Although you might want to order all your tasks, concentrating only on the high priority tasks avoids wasting time on ranking the whole list, which will change on a day-to-day basis.

4. *Delegated person [if any]* – where you make a decision as to whether you will progress the task yourself or allocate the task to someone else where possible. This effectively allows you to concentrate on the tasks that are more important to you, or where you have no time availability

to do it yourself, or where someone else is clearly a better option to do it. On the actual spreadsheet, you need only list names for tasks that are being delegated to others (and otherwise leave them blank).

You can ignore ordering delegation tasks if you are simply forwarding them; however, sometimes it is helpful to convey the level of urgency when passing them on to others.

Task Description	Priority	Order	Delegated Person
Attend interview for John Rogers			Simon
Complete Bates matter report	1	5 (or E)	
Apply for patent for Jane Andrews	1	3 (or C)	
Organize printing for AGM	1	1 (or A)	Mary
Submit award application for Ian			
Write speech for AGM opening	1	4 (or D)	
Make appointment with law society	1	2 (or B)	
Draft advert for new associate			
Arrange new firm logo redesign			
Renew arbitrator membership			

Figure 2: Urgency-driven approach.

The model will help you remain focused on achieving the "1" rated items and maintaining the discipline to doing them in the order you set. The challenge with this model is that important things may be delayed if you are only focused on urgent, and urgent and important tasks. This is where method 2 may be better.

Method 2 – Important to urgent approach

Think back to school or university where you forgot about an assignment until the last moment. The lack of time to complete it meant you generally worked faster and more efficiently to get it done. Basically, the less time you had, the less chance you had for procrastination, and the higher focus you maintained to ensure you met the deadline.

If you are given three days to complete a two-day task, it will typically take you three days. The concept is often referred to as "Parkinson's Law", where Cyril Northcote Parkinson wrote in a satirical essay published in *The*

Economist in 1955, that *"Work expands to fill the time available for its completion"*. It works on the premise that a person generally adapts their performance level to use the time they have available or is allocated, even though they may have otherwise worked faster given a tighter time frame.

Imagine you have three urgent tasks you know need to get done today. Method 2 considers the urgent, urgent and important, and the important but not urgent columns. In this way you could choose to do an important task before the urgent. This will give you less time to get the urgent done, and arguably you become more efficient in getting all the remaining urgent tasks done in the time left.

Method 2 makes sure you don't forget about the "important but non-urgent" tasks, as the "important" tasks are the ones that typically change your future. See Figure 3.

Task Description	Urgent	Important	Order	Delegated Person
Attend interview for John Rogers				Simon
Complete Bates matter report	1		2	
Apply for patent for Jane Andrews	1	1	1	
Organize printing for AGM	1		5	Mary
Submit award application for Ian				
Write speech for AGM opening				
Make appointment with law society		1	3	
Draft advert for new associate	1		4	
Arrange new firm logo redesign				
Renew arbitrator membership				

Figure 3: Important to urgent approach.

The model shows where a task is urgent and important, just urgent, or just important, and allows you to maintain the discipline to doing them in the order you set. Tasks that are urgent and important should take preference.

Method 3 – Eisenhower Matrix approach

Method 3 continues to build on Model 2 but purposely considers even the "not urgent and not important" tasks more thoroughly.

This popular method was based on former US president Dwight D.

Eisenhower's philosophy: *"What is important is seldom urgent and what is urgent is seldom important"*. He was known for his exceptional organizational and decision-making skills, particularly in World War II where he was appointed the Supreme Commander of the Allied Expeditionary Force and is attributed the architect of Allied victory in Western Europe.

It is based on dividing tasks into four groups (see Figure 4):
- *Urgent and important* – where it is suggested to do those tasks immediately.
- *Important but not urgent* – where the tasks should be planned and scheduled.
- *Urgent but not important* – where the tasks should be delegated to others where possible to allow you personally to focus on important tasks.
- *Neither urgent nor important* – where tasks may be later contemplated and often deleted.

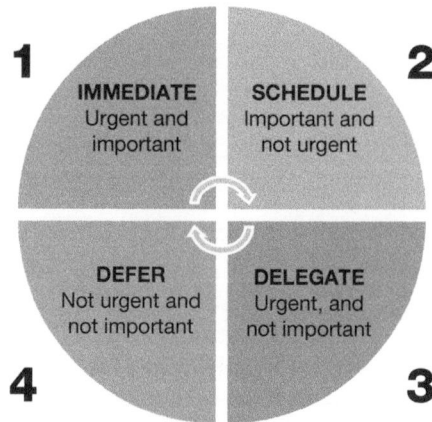

Figure 4: Based on the Eisenhower Matrix approach.

In practice, you typically need to have the following columns in your spreadsheet (see Figure 5 on the following page):
1. *Task description* – where column 1 has the task description listed.
2. *The four quadrants* – where columns 2 to 5 are based on the four categories of urgency and importance.
3. *Order the tasks* – where column 6 is the sequential order of the prioritized tasks to progress, with the priority based on ranking the:
   - Urgent and important first, with consideration to the urgent only;
   - Important next, to schedule;

- Urgent next with the intent to delegate; and
- The remainder.

4. *Delegated person* – where column 7 shows any delegated person.

This method makes it clearer as to the time and important sensitivity status of each task, with an emphasis on the important tasks.

Task Description	Urgent and Important	Important	Urgent	Neither Urgent or Important	Action Order	Delegated Person
Attend interview for John Rogers		X			6	Simon
Complete Bates matter report	X				2	
Apply for patent for Jane Andrews		X			7	
Organize printing for AGM	X				1	Mary
Submit award application for Ian				X	9	
Write speech for AGM opening		X			4	
Make appointment with Law Society				X	10	
Draft advert for new associate		X			5	
Arrange new firm logo redesign		X			8	
Renew investigation license			X		3	John

Figure 5: Applying the matrix.

Method 4 – Kanban approach

This method is considered a "lean" model and is often applied in an agile project management approach that emphasizes a simple workflow. It provides a visual display on the expected, progressing, and completed work. It is effective for delegating legal team work, as the total work is declared, and then allocated or accepted by a team member who then progresses it until it is complete.

The term "kanban" comes from Japan – 看 (kan) that means to look or watch, and 板 (ban) that means a board or card. It is a visual system for managing work that is either displayed on a wall or a software tool. It is used to trigger a team member to select their next work task. When used in a group setting, where the tasks are not specifically allocated to a person, individuals can effectively select the work they feel they can best undertake. This is a natural way of allocation as people tend to select tasks based on their natural behavioral style and interests (see Figure 6).

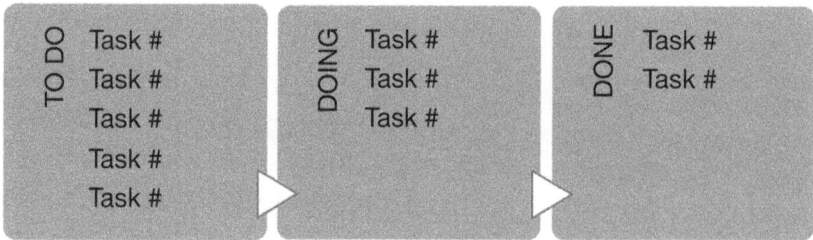

TO DO	DOING	DONE
Task #	Task #	Task #
Task #	Task #	Task #
Task #	Task #	
Task #		
Task #		

Figure 6: The Kanban approach.

It works by having a three-step workflow process where there is a column for work "to do", a column for work currently in progress that is defined as "doing", and a column for work completed that is defined as "done". Basically, the work is moved through the process, and ends on the task being acknowledged as completed.

The prioritization order can also be marked on the "to do" tasks, to avoid it serving solely as a self-prioritizing system managed by the team members who accept the tasks.

Method 5 – Using your calendar approach

Your calendar items, such as meetings, are generally tasks. Some packaged email systems allow for action lists and are integrated to allow for allocations through emails and reporting back on task progress.

If this tool is used to allocate time slots in your calendar for your prioritized tasks, it is a smart way to set a time constraint for each task. Otherwise, your action list is to guide the spare time between your calendar commitments.

Scheduling time can improve your productivity. For example, when you give yourself half an hour to do a task, you need to believe you only have half an hour, so you focus on getting it done within that timeslot, just like having an assignment deadline that you can't miss.

If you let yourself keep working through the end time – like ignoring a meeting end time and continuing with the meeting – your brain doesn't see the schedule as a real deadline. If you believe the time limit is real, you will try to push through the work in a focused manner. If you do not finish the task within the allocated time, you can put it down and start on the next scheduled task (remembering of course to schedule more time to complete it).

What tends to happen is that you want to finish the last outstanding uncompleted task. This will usually cause you to work more efficiently on the next task, with the intention of getting through it faster in order that you will have some spare time to go back and finish the last task. This is healthy pressure you can put on yourself, knowing that the end time is not really critical, but it keeps you performing even though in reality it is an estimated time block.

Method 6 – Issues priority approach

Going beyond simply prioritizing tasks in general, the "Pareto Principle" or "80/20 Rule" model focuses on the key issue areas that have the most issues.

Vilfredo Pareto, an Italian economist and socialist, started to observe a pattern that has now been applied to many applications, that started from his insight that approximately 80 percent of the land in Italy was owned by 20 percent of the population. This was seen as a generic pattern that could be applied to many statistics as a general rule of thumb. Its popularity was believed to be accelerated by Dr Joseph Moses Juran, who was a quality management pioneer, who started seeing the relationship in many facets of business.

This 80/20 rule can apply to many aspects of law firm operations as a general rule of thumb, such as 80 percent of sales revenue comes from 20 percent of clients, or 80 percent of product sales comes from 20 percent of the product range.

For the purpose of solving issues, the principle would imply that 80 percent of issues comes from only 20 percent of the category of issues. If you are therefore focused on remediating those issues in the 20 percent categories, you will solve 80 percent of the issues. However, the most important issue may lie in the 80 percent categories area, so that has to be considered.

Where a legal team maintains an issues register (particularly relevant to legal project management in managing matters or internal improvement projects) then by categorizing each issue, the quantity of issues against each category can be plotted into a graph, and it may become evident that 80 percent of the issues are in only a small portion of categories (see Figure 7).

This approach can help companies like Microsoft and Apple to manage a product release, despite having a large amount of software bugs. By categorizing the software bugs, and then focusing on the 20 percent, they can release an update to make it a more stable product. Once complete, they can then recategorize the remaining bugs, and focus on the next 20 percent, and repeat the process. The numbers suggest that this prioritization method can help bring down the quantity of issues dramatically.

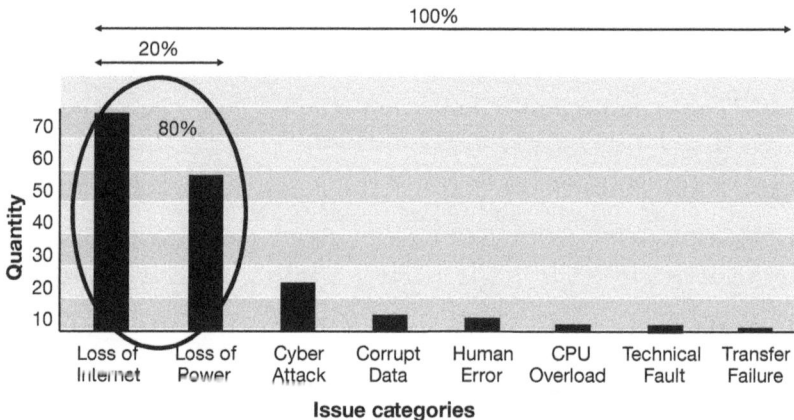

Figure 7: Issues register.

Imagine starting with 65,000 known bugs, and applying this process:
1. 65,000 software bugs are reduced to only 13,000 (20 percent).
2. 13,000 remaining software bugs are then reduced to only 2,600 (20 percent).
3. 2,600 remaining software bugs are then reduced to only 520 (20 percent).

This becomes an impressive method of focusing on the main causes where the majority of issues reside. It allows for a focus on reducing the quantity of issues as quickly as possible. This is a value-driven method of identifying the best investment in time.

Step 3: Delegate – allocating tasks to the right people

Based on your own workload level and availability, you may need to delegate tasks to other team members who are more suitably skilled. Effective teams will have people with differing behavioral styles that bring synergy to the group. What one person finds easy to do, a person with their opposite style will find harder to do, and vice versa.

When you are operating in your core behavioral strength you are in what neuroscience calls a "state of flow", where tasks can be done faster, more effectively, and with greater enjoyment. This state uses less energy and therefore you can get much more work done. It is likened to swimming downstream and having the current carrying you. Conversely, if you had a behavioral style that was opposite, that same task would be in your "ebb" and would feel like you were swimming against the current. You would ultimately give up, avoid the task, or get frustrated.

You need to develop your natural talents so that they are high skills. Whilst you are born with a natural potential talent based on your behavioral style, you have to develop your growth potential to a high state of performance. Popularized by Malcolm Gladwell in his book *Outliers: The Story of Success*, the idea is it takes approximately 10,000 hours of deliberate practice to achieve a level of mastery, known as the "Ten-Hour Rule". It was based on the earlier research of psychologist Anders Ericsson who suggested this was more of an average; however, it makes sense if the topic of mastery is aligned to their natural behavioral style.

If you were to carry out a behavioral profile on the people featured in the research study, it is likely those achieving mastery were undertaking an activity aligned to their natural talents, and as their skills developed (from potential to actual), the state of flow was achieved. This is likely as people normally stick with an activity they have an interest in (passion), where they see improvement (growth), and they do the activity long enough to be eligible for such research where they are performing (the state of flow). Conversely, if a person's behavioral profile is not aligned to that topic of mastery, they would have given up much earlier, so they never become a part of the research. If they did persist, they would likely become proficient at the task, but would not excel in it or enjoy it. This is due to the level of energy that is used when in an ebb state.

This means there are four quadrants when considering your behavioral style strengths:

1. *Growth* – natural talents that need to be developed (growth potential).
2. *Flow state* – natural talents that have been developed that now are high skills that use the least energy.
3. *Limited skill* – non-natural talents that you have developed to a level of proficiency.
4. *Ebb* – the opposite of your natural talents that use the most energy.

It follows, therefore, that different behavioral styles find different tasks easier and harder. What you don't like to do, based on your behavioral style, your opposite team member may well find enjoyable. They can do it faster and easier than you, as opposed to the time-consuming effort and frustration you would feel for progressing the same task. This encourages the use of behavioral profiling for all team members.

You are cautioned not to delegate tasks that are within your own flow state where possible (unless workload or availability demands it), as that would take the enjoyment out of your work, and all the benefits of getting things done with the least amount of energy that gives you a sense of accomplishment. Those very tasks make you successful.

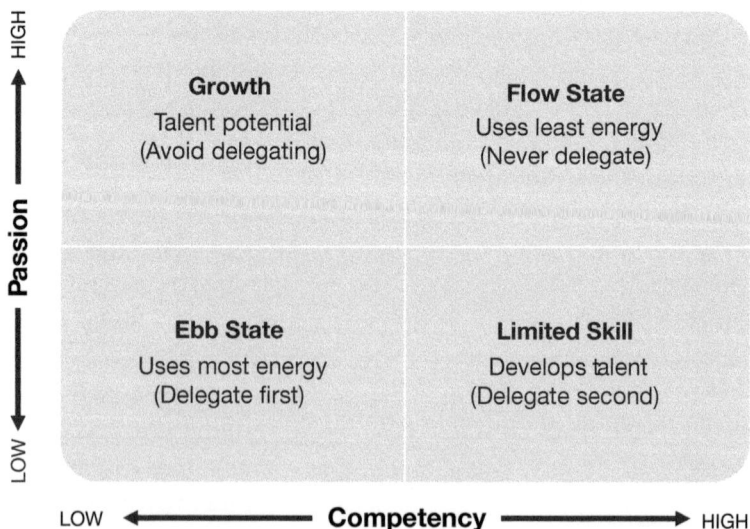

	HIGH	
Growth		**Flow State**
Talent potential		Uses least energy
(Avoid delegating)		(Never delegate)
Ebb State		**Limited Skill**
Uses most energy		Develops talent
(Delegate first)		(Delegate second)
	LOW	

Passion — LOW ↔ HIGH

LOW ← **Competency** → HIGH

Figure 8: The four quadrants of behavioral style.

Some people, not knowing better, have persisted through their ebb state to increase competency to a limited skill or proficiency level. The question is, how many people do you know that are reasonable at their job, but hate it? These people are living on the lower part of this matrix (low passion area). It is likely many people are living like this, struggling, without even realizing their hard life relates to their low energy state from working in the wrong role or at least doing it in an inappropriate way. If they moved to align their role and the majority of their job tasks to utilize their natural talents and ensure their talents were developed, they would ultimately get to their flow state and realize their mastery opportunity.

This then makes delegation easy, as you:
1. Delegate your ebb-related tasks that takes your energy away first;
2. Delegate those tasks where you have limited skills that are not alligned to your passions;
3. Avoid delegating those tasks that will enhance your growth potential; and
4. Never delegate your flow-aligned tasks (unless purposeful).

Behavioral profiling tools provide a fast-track method to understanding your natural and non-natural styles. The DISC behavioral model, created in 1928 by Dr William Moulton Marston in his book *Emotions of Norman People*, is the most common behavioral model. For context, Dr Marston defined DISC to represent four quadrants where:
1. The Driver profile is an extrovert and has a task orientated style.
2. The Influencer profile is highly extroverted and has a people orientated style.
3. The Stable profile is an introvert and has a people orientated style.
4. The Compliance profile is highly introverted and has a task orientated style.

Figure 9 shows an example of an individual's "Natural Style", noting that an individual can have one, two, or three traits that make up their behavioral style or behavioral blend. In this example, the person is known to have an SC behavioral style.

The traits above the midline (Neutral level) highlight what they are, and the traits below the midline indicate what they are not. The traits most distant from the midline indicate what would likely be observable to others. This can highlight challenges between their current performance and their potential performance, as ideally the graphs would be the same if the individual was performing "in flow", where they would be living their natural style and reaping the benefits.

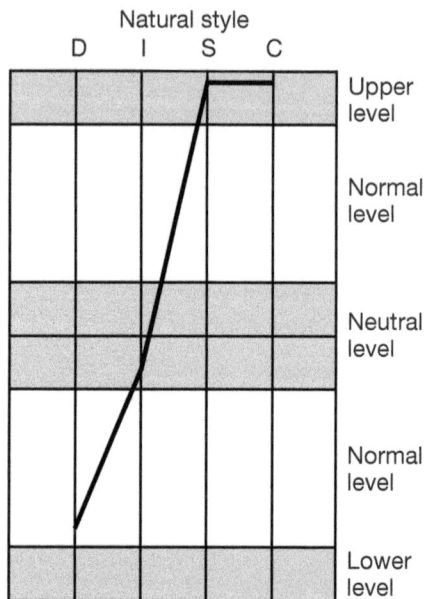

Figure 9: Plotting an individual's "natural style".

Figure 10 then looks at the need to adjust, in order to carry out a particular role successfully. If the profile is accurate, the "Natural Style" (on the right) should not change, as it is indicative of the natural style the person is born with. The "Perceived Need to Adjust" (on the left) represents their adapted behaviors that reflect the current way they are using their profile traits, based on the role they are in. The analysis can therefore indicate what the person is currently doing (left), which in this case shows that both their core traits are either being underutilized or have not been developed fully. Each position of the individual traits has a meaning that can help provide insights as to how the person can change to become more productive. The aim is to have their perceived need to adjust (adapted style) in alignment with the natural style to be "in flow", where they would be living their natural style, and reaping the benefits.

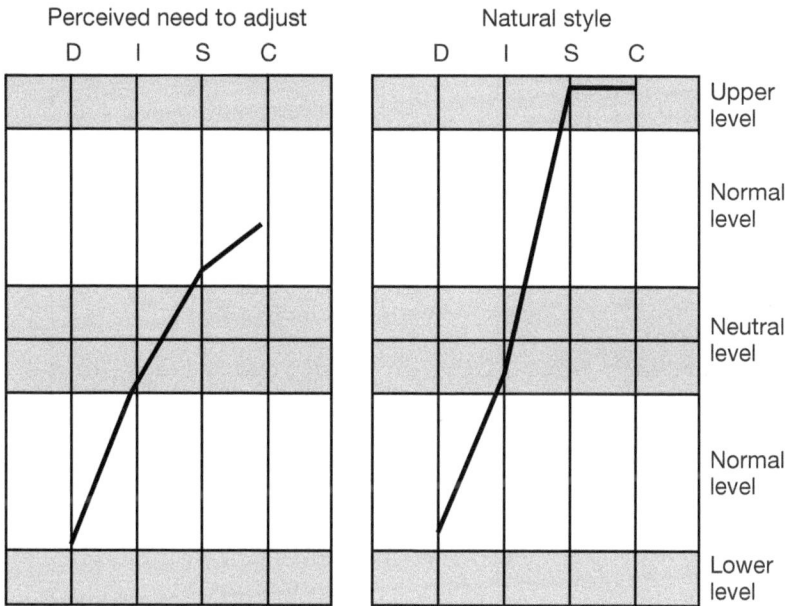

Figure 10: The perceived need to adjust.

The most impressive graph using the Extended DISC® profile identifies your flow and ebb points and shows the absolute point of your flow (see Figure 11). It is shown in the darkest shaded point, with the next shade indicating what the person has developed, and the lightest shade what they have not yet mastered. If an arrow appears, it indicates a misalignment of their energy. Basically, their natural skills are in the colored graph areas, and the white areas represent more ebb. Figure 11 indicates that a DI style person would be their ideal complimentary team member.

Behavioral profiles highlight the blend of behaviors within individuals. In a team setting, it's likely that multiple members will have strengths in areas where others may not, especially in the "white space" of another colleague's profile. This underscores the value of using behavioral tools to build teams strategically – matching members in a way that supports high performance. It also helps identify who is best suited to take on specific tasks.

It's important to remember that our thinking drives our behaviors and actions, which ultimately determine our results. This thinking is shaped by our values and beliefs – such as culture, religion, biases, and attitudes. So, while behavioral profiles are strong indicators of potential performance, they don't tell the whole story. A person may have excellent experience, qualifi-

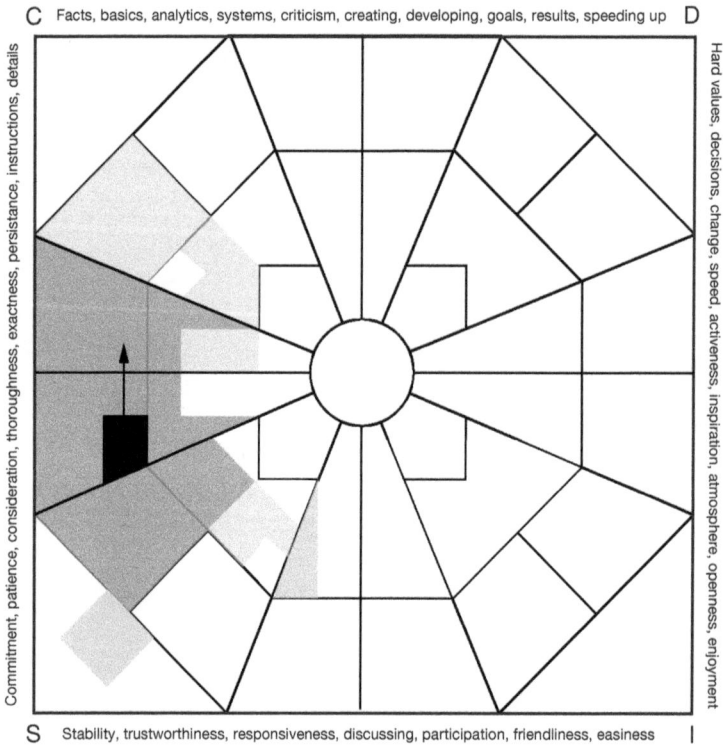

Figure 11: Extended DISC profile.

cations, and skills, but a poor attitude can undermine the benefits they bring to a team.

Step 4: Progress – aligning work to energy cycles for maximum productivity

Now that we have explored when to set priorities, methods on how to prioritize, and how delegation can be most effective, we can explore how to allocate certain tasks to specific times of the day to increase your overall productivity to get more work done.

They say that procrastination is the thief of time. It delays tasks getting done and can cause you to work on unproductive activities. To understand why high performers tend to procrastinate less than others, and why they seemingly get more work done in a day, we need to appreciate how individual energy flow works.

Although behavioral science explains that a person's natural behavioral style does influence their decisiveness in decision making and risk taking, the level of detail they like to delve into, and the amount of desired interaction with others they prefer, the first focal point should be on individual circadian rhythms that drive natural energy levels, as this indicates the times when they can get the maximum work done.

Your natural body rhythm is regulated by the suprachiasmatic nucleus in the hypothalamus within the brain, and represents your 24-hour internal clock, influencing your sleep–wake cycle and many other physical, mental, and behavioral processes. Although it is affected by external factors such as light, and neurochemistry like melatonin, which causes you to feel sleepy, it influences many factors including your body temperature, hormones, digestion, and mental state. It also drives your high energy, low energy, and dips in energy throughout the day.

This explains why people often associate themselves as being a morning, afternoon, or night person, where they sense the time of day when their highest energy level is most evident. In reality, you are constantly depleting your energy, so when you feel high energy, you are operating using the least energy. This is your "state of flow", where you can get tasks done faster, more efficiently, and with more enjoyment.

Interestingly, high performers often struggle to identify which periods of time represent their high energy cycle that will be explored – as they are simply doing something different than other people. This includes the quality of their sleep.

Trying to do complex tasks at low energy levels is linked to low motivation or disinterest, which can lead to procrastination. Procrastination can arise from many other factors, including a lack of process or tools in identifying and categorizing goals, or being drawn to do more fun activities that provide faster neurochemical rewards (which explains why using social media tends to give instant gratification). The result is avoiding the harder tasks.

Aligning tasks with consideration to your circadian rhythm can help you get more work accomplished. Depending on how you structure your schedule, it can seemingly give you more productive time in your day. Take a look at Figure 12, which shows an example of a morning person whose energy levels peak soon after they wake up, and then start to move to a lower energy state in the afternoon, leading to when they shows an example of a sleep.

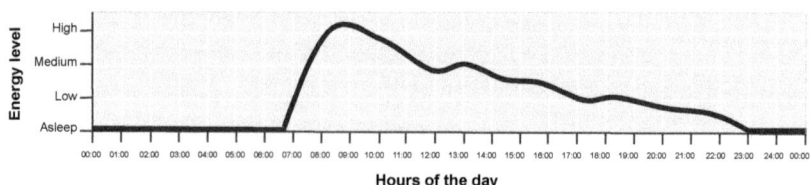

Figure 12: Energy levels throughout the day – the morning person.

When you are feeling good (your high energy state), you tend to do fun activities and naturally avoid the hard work activities. When you then go to do those difficult tasks at low energy level times, it feels too hard and you think, *"Oh, I will do this tomorrow"* and put it off. This is where procrastination occurs. This is due to the high energy state being where your brain is most active and where you should undertake the most complex tasks.

If you change your routine so you only do the difficult, hard, and complex work when in your high energy zone, then you won't procrastinate, or at least not as much, and you will be able to tackle those brain draining tasks much easier and faster, doing them better than at any other time of the day. You are effectively exercising the brain when you do this and will be able to get the most out of your time.

One hour of hard work in your high energy period has been found to take much longer to do than the same work in your low energy period, sometimes reportedly double the time than in a high energy period. Although this sounds obvious, you will realize that in doing this, you will achieve a lot more work in a workday as a result. This of course needs to be aligned with doing the right work, and that is where task prioritization comes in.

In your low energy state, doing hard work makes no sense as you will struggle. This is why you tend to turn to the tasks you find more enjoyable. When you do work that is more aligned with your passions, you will see your energy levels seemingly rise. Consider when you come home exhausted from work and a friend contacts you about doing one of your favorite activities. Suddenly your excitement drives your sense of energy up, and you find you are raring to go. This is a neurochemical response when you align yourself with your passions, making you feel like you have more energy.

The concept of "passions" is not what makes you jump out of bed excited – rather it includes activities that are aligned to your natural behavioral style that are easy for you to do. Look to those tasks that other people approach you to help them with, as they are recognizing your talents.

The boost in motivational neurochemicals is likened to taking some form of wonder drug, and you now feel energized. Your overall higher energy state brings more productivity. Even as you get through the hard work, the achievement neurochemicals kick in, and you have a high sense of accomplishment.

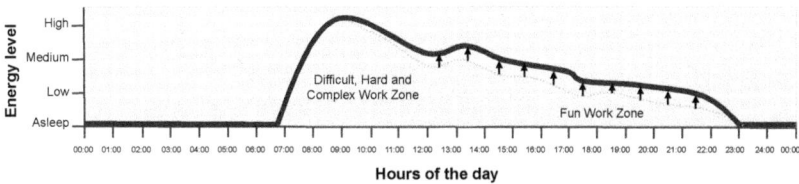

Figure 13: Energy levels throughout the day – considering fun activities.

You have now pushed through the initial low energy phase. This means that you get more done when you consider your energy level appears to have risen.

Two interesting observations about high performers – they tend to procrastinate less, and they tend to not know as clearly if they are a morning, afternoon or night person. The first is explained by switching the difficult tasks and the fun activities that caused them to have the energy to progress work, leading to less procrastination. The second is explained when you observe that when energy levels rise in your low energy zone, the differential between high and low energy levels is not so obvious.

Your quality of sleep is also important and can increase when considering the impacts of aligning to your energy cycle. When you are "brain dead" from working the brain, you may find it difficult to sleep as your body may still feel energized, effectively keeping you awake. Similarly, when your body feels "dead tired", but your brain is active, you also have trouble sleeping.

Now, imagine structuring your day so that you do your most difficult, complex tasks during your high-energy periods – exercising the mind – and reserve lighter, more enjoyable activities for when your energy is lower. These lighter tasks often involve some movement, helping to exercise the body. By the end of the day, both mind and body are ready for rest, leading to better sleep quality.

Interestingly, when you live this way, you may begin to notice your natural sleep duration. Most people tend to sleep between 7.5 and 8.5 hours per night. For example, if you go to bed at 9pm and wake at 5am, you're likely an eight-hour sleeper. If you go to bed at 9.30pm, you may wake naturally at 5.30am, and so on. Once you identify your natural sleep cycle, it's important to maintain it – sleeping less than your optimal duration can lead to sleep deprivation.

When you get quality sleep, you wake up feeling energized, and the cycle continues. This shows that how you structure your workday – aligned with your circadian rhythm – directly affects how much you achieve and how efficiently your brain and body perform.

The process that influences your most productive self follows three steps:

1. You undertake the difficult, hard, and complex tasks at your highest energy level, where you work most efficiently and can progress many more tasks than at any other time of the day. This is where your mind gets exercised and the majority of your work gets progressed.
2. You undertake the fun tasks at your lowest energy level, which will raise your sense of low energy and still allow you to progress less complex work. This is where your body gets exercised.
3. When you go to sleep, having exercised both the mind and body, the quality of sleep from your now evident natural sleeping cycle refreshes and renews you, to take on a new day.

If your schedule is largely something you can control, you can prioritize your work to take into account making yourself available for work tasks at high energy periods. Take the case of the sole lawyer who is a morning person, involved in visiting clients as a means of business development, who also has to do their own invoicing. They may be an extrovert and enjoy catching up with clients, but find the detailed task of invoicing painful and something they tend to avoid.

As a morning person, they should do the invoicing first, giving them a sense of achievement and leaving them to move on to smashing through client work during the rest of their high energy zone. In the afternoon, as their energy levels drop, visiting clients would be their fun activity. They are now far more productive across the day, getting through work easier, and better enjoying their job. They can block out time in their calendar to do the hard work in the mornings and avoid meetings so they can be working on tasks to get the most work completed possible throughout their day.

In conclusion

Many people use a prioritization system yet still struggle with productivity. We've explored how aligning your work with your natural circadian rhythms and behavioral styles can address this challenge. Considering how much time and energy you invest in your work, you deserve to enjoy it. That enjoyment comes from having an effective system that helps you focus on the tasks that deliver the highest return on your time. By aligning this system with your natural rhythm, behavioral style, and individual strengths, you begin working in a way that suits you best. This shift can be transformative – leading to not only higher and more purposeful productivity, but also greater satisfaction in your work.

Chapter 2:
The high-value lawyer – focusing on what matters most

By David Skinner and Karen Dunn Skinner, co-founders, Gimbal Consulting

The real cost of doing it all

It starts out small. You tell yourself it's just one more task – answering a client email, processing a retainer, formatting a letter, chasing down an overdue invoice. But over time, those little things add up. Before you know it, your entire day has been spent on tasks that don't require your legal expertise.

Sound familiar?

If you're like most lawyers, your to-do list is a combination of client work, admin, marketing, finance, tech, HR, and a dozen other responsibilities you never imagined you'd be juggling when you went to law school. You're constantly busy but not necessarily productive. You're working hard but not always on the right things. The irony is, the longer you keep trying to do everything, the further you get from the success you want, whether that's financial freedom, work–life balance, or simply enjoying the work you do.

Let me tell you about "Vivian", a client from our coaching work. Vivian runs a small family law litigation boutique. When she came to us, she was working over 60 hours a week but only billing 20. Apart from attending court, most of her time during normal business hours was consumed by intake calls, email follow-ups, and tech glitches. She couldn't work on her briefs, motions, and arguments until after her son was in bed. She was overwhelmed and burning out. She resented working long hours and missing family dinners, social engagements, and holidays. She felt she was letting everyone down – her clients, her colleagues, her friends, and, perhaps most importantly, her family.

This chapter is about helping you avoid Vivian's situation by learning how to focus on what truly matters and delegate the rest. This is about more than time management. It's about building a profitable, sustainable practice you love, and getting your life back.

The high-value work only you can do

Not all work is created equal. Some tasks create more impact, income, and opportunity than others. The key is identifying which tasks fall into that high-value category and making them *your* priority.

Your high-value work is the work you're uniquely qualified to do. It might be negotiating complex agreements, shaping firm strategy, building relationships and developing new business, or mentoring your rising stars. It doesn't have to generate immediate revenue to be "high-value". It can be anything that adds value to your business, including your legal expertise, experience, leadership, business acumen, or reputation. It's where your skill, value, and passion align, and it's where your time delivers the greatest return for you, your firm, and, ultimately, your clients, regardless of whether it generates revenue in the moment.

This intersection between what you're uniquely qualified to do, the work you love doing, and the work that adds the greatest value is your "Power Zone". When you're operating in your Power Zone, you're at your peak in terms of output and satisfaction. You're doing work that energizes you and delivers results for your clients and your firm.

The problem is that most lawyers spend much of their time doing everything other than focusing on work in their Power Zone. We regularly see lawyers screening potential new clients, drowning in email correspondence, fixing typos and formatting errors, answering routine client questions, and playing dueling schedules with colleagues, clients, and opposing counsel. Though important, these are not high-value tasks, at least not for you.

To start the shift into your Power Zone, ask yourself:

- What are the top five things I do that actually move the needle in my practice?
- Which tasks energize me and make me feel like I'm doing meaningful work?
- What would happen if I spent 80 percent of my time on those tasks?

If you want to take it further, try this "Post-it Party" exercise.

1. Grab a pile of sticky notes and write down everything you did during the past seven days (yes, seven, because if you're like most of the lawyers we know, you probably do some work most weekends). Nothing is too insignificant to capture. If you did it, write it down. Record one task per note. Paste them on a wall, a window, or a door.
2. Stand back, review, reflect on, and then sort the stickies into one of the following four categories:

- *Quadrant 1:* Things you are uniquely qualified to do by virtue of your legal expertise and experience, some other qualification, your ownership of or leadership position in the firm.
- *Quadrant 2:* Things you really don't enjoy that someone else could do better, faster, and/or cheaper than you.
- *Quadrant 3:* Things you do enjoy that someone else could do better, faster, and/or cheaper than you.
- *Quadrant 4:* Things that don't add any value to the firm or its clients and you should stop doing altogether.

3. Focusing only on the tasks that fall into Quadrant 1, look for the overlap where the tasks are (mostly) enjoyable, high value, and uniquely yours. That's your Power Zone.

Another coaching client, "Sanjay", is the founder and managing partner at a thriving employment firm. Given his position, he's responsible for much more than delivering revenue-generating services to clients. His Power Zone includes establishing the firm's vision, strategic objectives, and financial and performance goals; acting as a mentor, advisor, and sounding board to his colleagues; and developing new business and managing relations with the firm's most important clients.

What's not in his Power Zone is managing his email inbox. He'd open his email tab to handle one specific message, only to get distracted by other unrelated, sometimes entirely unimportant emails, and suddenly find he'd lost an hour of time.

By delegating management of his inbox to an assistant, he recovered more than two hours every day, time he now applies directly to work that *is* in his Power Zone.

Watch for these warning signs that you're not focused on your Power Zone:

- You're always busy, often behind, and driven by urgency.
- You struggle to get to the important client-facing work.
- You frequently write down or write off time because you can't justify the cost, given the value of the work delivered.
- You feel like you're the only one who can make things happen.
- Your to-do list never gets any shorter.
- Your utilization rate (the average number of hours you bill per day divided by the average number of hours you're "at" work) is less than 50 percent.

Even if you enjoy a particular task, if someone else could do it better, faster, and/or cheaper than you, you're wasting time. And time is your scarcest and most valuable resource, especially when your goal is to *make every six minutes count.*

Being in your Power Zone isn't just good for business, it's good for you. It's where you do your most rewarding, fulfilling work. Happy people are more productive, and happy leaders are better leaders.

Don't let urgency determine how you prioritize your to-do list

If you're using a single, undifferentiated to-do list to manage your day, there's a good chance you're prioritizing based on urgency, not importance. This is a trap.

Many lawyers spend their days putting out fires – answering the loudest client, responding to the most recent email, tackling whatever is due today. That's urgency. It feels productive because you're always busy. But being busy isn't the same as being effective or productive, and it certainly doesn't mean you're being profitable.

Prioritization means separating the urgent from the important. One helpful tool here is the Eisenhower Matrix, a 2×2 matrix with Important/Not Important on one axis and Urgent/Not Urgent on the other, creating a grid made up of four sectors (see chapter 1 for more on this). Here are some examples to illustrate the point. Your matrix will depend on your role, your work, and your circumstances:

- *Sector 1 – Important but Not Urgent* (top left): Preparing for a regularly scheduled meeting with a keynote client, strategic planning, marketing and business development.
- *Sector 2 – Important and Urgent* (top right): Impending deadlines, unforeseen emergencies, court appearances, obtaining a conflicts waiver.
- *Sector 3 – Not Important and Not Urgent* (bottom left): Attending meetings where your presence isn't required, checking website analytics for SEO performance, organizing digital files in your document management system.
- *Sector 4 – Not Important but Urgent* (bottom right): Most interruptions, emails from clients requesting updates that a junior could handle, booking travel or handling scheduling issues.

Most lawyers live in Sectors 2 and 4 where everything is "urgent". Sometimes, working in Sector 2 (Important and Urgent) is inevitable. High-stakes client crises, a rush to meet a court deadline, or some strategic firm decision that requires your immediate attention will arise from time to time, and you'll have to do what you have to do. That's business.

However, urgency shouldn't be the basis upon which your to-do list is prioritized. If it is, the reactive, often fragmented nature of your practice may explain why you feel overwhelmed and stuck in the "just one more thing" mode.

Instead, when you prioritize tasks that are important but *not* urgent, you gain control over your schedule. You can proactively allocate your time to high-value, strategic activities rather than constantly reacting to (usually other people's) crises. There's less mental and emotional strain, allowing you to invest more energy in the things that matter most within your Power Zone.

By focusing on your Power Zone – maybe on deep legal analysis, high-stakes negotiation, or cultivating client relationships and developing business – you generate more value for each hour (whether billable or not) you spend working.

You're able to focus, getting more of the important work done in less time. You free up time to knock other things off your to-do list or spend time in your community, with family, and/or friends. And that brings us back to the value of being happy. The option to do other things that enrich your life either professionally or personally is, frankly, priceless.

It always amazes us how many lawyers waste time on tasks that fall into Sector 3 of the Eisenhower Matrix – work that is neither important nor urgent – despite the common complaint that there isn't enough time to get everything done in the day. Often there's a simple misunderstanding that leads to this misallocation of time.

For example, during a process improvement project, we discovered a relationship partner was investing time each month preparing a report for one of his general counsel clients. He believed the report – a status update on all the open matters the firm was handling for the client's legal department – was important. He was surprised to learn that not only was the report not of any value to the GC, whose own team was already keeping him abreast of each matter being handled by external counsel, but the monthly report was also a source of irritation. The GC felt obliged to read the report even though he considered it superfluous; after all, he was paying for it. A simple misunderstanding of what was important led to an inappropriate prioritization, so the partner wasted his time, and the GC was having his time wasted.

Preparing that monthly report fits firmly in Sector 3 – it was neither urgent nor important. Indeed, since it wasn't delivering any value to the client, this wasn't a task that needed to be completed at all. Doing away with the report saved both parties valuable time, and the GC stopped paying for a report that delivered no value.

As much as possible, prioritize work that falls into Sector 1 of the Eisenhower Matrix. That's your Power Zone and it's where the magic happens. The work is important – however you define important – but it's not urgent. You have the luxury of making intentional decisions that build a better practice – a practice you love, doing work you're uniquely qualified to do that generates high value for the firm. The time you save when you're not distracted by other people's urgencies can be reinvested in ways you feel are most beneficial. Maybe that's high-value client work, or maybe it's getting out of the office and recharging your batteries. Practicing a hobby, doing exercise, or spending time with family and friends will help you better focus on your Power Zone, be a better lawyer and a better leader when you're at the office (see chapter 10 for more on this).

Use this strategy to shift time into your Sector 1 priorities:

- *Block it.* Protect time in your calendar for the higher-value work that's in your Power Zone. It's harder to accomplish mission-critical work (whether immediately revenue-generating or not) if you haven't made time for it.
- *Track it.* Whether you bill by the hour or work with fixed fees, you should still track your time, so you know how much time you spend on the important but non-urgent work that makes up your Power Zone. You can't adjust your work and time allocation if you don't know your baseline.
- *Guard it.* Set boundaries with team members and clients so the time you've set aside to focus on your Sector 1 priorities isn't interrupted.

This isn't just about time management – it's about energy and attention. Your highest-value work requires focus, not multitasking.

Here's a quick exercise:

- Pick five tasks from your to-do list.
- Use the Eisenhower Matrix to determine the priority of each.
- Choose one "important but not urgent" task (Sector 1) to protect this week, block the time you think you'll need across the week to complete it, and at the appointed time each day close your door, turn off your notifications, and focus fully on that task.

Many people are pretty good about using their calendar to protect the time already available for Power Zone work. Instead, their challenge is creating the space to spend more time there, and that's where delegation comes in.

Delegation – the superpower you're not using

Delegation isn't laziness. It's not giving away work because you don't feel like doing it. Nor is it abdicating control or responsibility. Delegation is an invaluable strategy that frees up your most valuable resource – your time – so you can use it more effectively, productively, and profitably on things within your Power Zone.

Still, many lawyers resist delegation. They think:

- "It'll take too long to explain."
- "I can do it faster myself."
- "I can't afford to hire someone."

These common objections are a product of short-term thinking. Sustainable delegation requires time, but that time is an investment in efficiency, sanity, and success. Done right, it can start paying dividends immediately.

"It'll take too long to explain."
Believing you're too busy to explain a task to someone is a warning. Yes, it will take time to write down and explain the process your delegate must follow, but when you're done, you'll never have to do that task again yourself. Assuming you aren't delegating a one-off task, the time you save will accrue to your benefit in perpetuity. It's hard to argue you don't have time to teach someone a routine task that requires 30 minutes a day when you'll save 2.5 hours each week for the rest of your practicing career!

"I can do it faster myself."
If the task you're delegating isn't in your Power Zone, then it's doubtful you can do it faster. There are almost always lower-cost resources with more appropriate training than you who can do the task faster and at least as well as you. How fast and how well may also be a function of the resources (the instructions, checklist, practice guide, and/or precedent) you provide. And even if the delegate takes longer, the time you save not doing it can be allocated to higher-value tasks that others can't complete. There will always be a net benefit.

"I can't afford to hire someone."

Yes, you can. Look at the options and then do the math.

First, without going into the benefits of delegating to technology through workflow automation, nothing says you have to hire a full- or part-time "employee" (with all the labor and tax costs associated with adding to your payroll). The pandemic taught us all how to navigate lower-cost contractors working remotely or in a hybrid manner.

As for the math, let's assume you currently spend two hours a day on business and administrative tasks that someone other than you could do better, faster, and/or cheaper, even though some initial training may be required. Remember Sanjay? He was wasting two hours every day getting distracted by his email.

Multiply your hourly rate, say $500/hour, by the two hours you're currently spending on those tasks. If you charge a flat fee, let's assume that your notional hourly rate – calculated by dividing the flat fee you charge for a matter by the approximate number of hours you spend working on the matter – is the same.

You're leaving approximately $1,000 of revenue on the table every day you do two hours of business and administrative tasks that fall outside your Power Zone. You can certainly find someone else to do that same work for far less than $500/hour. The time you save can then be invested in tasks that *are* in your Power Zone.

The math doesn't lie. The business case for delegating is obvious and compelling. Indeed, you can't afford *not* to hire someone to do many of the routine business and administrative tasks that are preventing you from focusing on priorities in your Power Zone.

Let's highlight this with an example. The dispute resolution team at one of our client firms was constantly swamped with work. Collections wasn't in the practice group leader's Power Zone. Because he neither liked nor excelled at collections calls, the team had a lot of overdue accounts receivable.

The firm hired a virtual assistant to create and then manage an entire process around collections.

The benefits have been significant. Not only is the virtual assistant covering her cost many times over with the overdue accounts receivable she's regularly collecting, she also has time to relieve the practice group leader of other tasks that aren't in his Power Zone. His overall productivity and profitability have increased, while his stress and overwhelm have decreased.

When it's done right, delegation doesn't relinquish your control over your operations, it builds your capacity.

For delegation to work, you need clear processes that empower your delegate to master the task with a minimum of interruptions and supervision. Our mantra here is, "Train, trust (and verify), and then let go".

Here's an easy framework for creating standard operating procedures (SOPs):

1. The next time you do a task you'd like to delegate, track every step as you do it. Include names of people and other resources involved and how to access them. Use Loom, Zoom, or another screen capture tool to record steps in technology platforms.

2. Organize and summarize the steps into an SOP. Create a clear and concise checklist or practice guide and include links to any video screen captures and relevant resources.

3. Test the accuracy of your SOP by following it to the letter the very next time you must do the same task.

4. If you don't get the result you intended, identify what's missing. Maybe you left out instructions for something you thought was obvious or intuitive. If it's not in your SOP, your delegate also won't get the right result, so revise it.

5. Finally, teach the process to your delegate. Accept that they may not complete the task perfectly the first few times they execute it. Provide constructive feedback and refine the SOP further as needed.

Most failures in delegation are a direct result of incomplete or inaccurate instructions from the delegator, not the delegate's lack of ability, so take the time to get your SOP right.

Think of each delegation as building a mini-process. Over time, you will build a solid library of SOPs and a practice that runs smoothly – even when (or precisely because) you're not the one pushing every button.

When you stop doing everything yourself, particularly the things that are outside your Power Zone, you create the leverage to grow and scale faster by liberating time to do other things you value.

Effective delegation also creates space for more strategy, better leadership, and innovation. It helps declutter your mental space by reducing distractions. When you stop micromanaging and empower team members to take on more responsibility, they grow in confidence and skill. You don't just get your time back, you build a more capable, resilient team supporting a much stronger firm.

Delegation gets you out of the grind into your Power Zone, doing work you love and creating real value. That's energizing!

In short, delegation is the foundation of a successful business that also provides the freedom to enjoy your life.

If that's not a superpower, we don't know what is.

When, what, and to whom – smarter delegation

Once you understand the power of delegation, the next step is to decide when to delegate, what to delegate, and who to delegate to.

On the question of *when to delegate*, the short answer is that it's never too early. Start now. Block off time in your calendar to work a little bit each day over the coming weeks to complete the practical exercises and steps outlined in this chapter. Set a date by which you'll hand over responsibility for a task that's outside your Power Zone and hold yourself to that implementation date.

As for *what to delegate*, start with this filter:

- Does the task require your legal expertise? In other words, is it in your Power Zone?
- Do you enjoy doing it?
- Would you pay someone your billable rate to do it?

If you answer "no" to any of these questions, that task is a strong candidate for delegation.

Start small. Begin with a lower-risk administrative task like setting dates for meetings and managing your calendar, organizing emails and ridding your inbox of unsolicited promotions from vendors and spam, or following up with clients on overdue invoices. These take up time but certainly don't require your attention.

As you gain confidence in your ability to delegate sustainably, your team proves itself, and you start freeing up time, you can invest some of that time creating SOPs for more complex tasks that more directly impact your practice. Think client intake, creating an initial draft of certain documents, preparing exhibit lists, or updating standard form documents. Supported by an appropriate SOP, each of these could be handed off to a law clerk, paralegal, or assistant.

When deciding *to whom to delegate* a task, determine the knowledge and skills required, look at the Power Zones of the people currently on your team, and if none is a likely candidate, consider outsourcing the task.

However, delegation isn't just limited to people. Technology can systematize and automate tasks like scheduling appointments, sending reminders, handling intake, generating invoices, and following up as payment dates approach and/or pass. If your systems are not integrated, there are tools that allow you to connect systems and create workflows across different apps.

Increasingly, lawyers are using AI to summarize large volumes of data and other information, including client meetings, to generate first drafts of client memoranda, court briefs, transaction and other documents. This is another form of delegation to technology.

You already bear responsibility for the work-product created by students, interns, law clerks, paralegals, and junior lawyers. Having to also review the output from AI is no different. It's certainly not a reason to eschew AI, particularly when the output can be generated in seconds rather than in the hours or days it might take a human.

People who aren't learning to use AI properly are increasingly at a competitive (and financial) disadvantage to those who are. And even if you're wary of accepting its help with the practice of law, there is so much that AI can do to support you in the business of law.

Smarter delegation is not just about liberating time to focus on work in your Power Zone by getting things off your plate. It's also about aligning the right work with the right person (or tool), so your whole practice (and business) operates more efficiently.

The time you could get back

Let's talk numbers. If you reclaim just one hour a day through delegation, that's five hours per week, 240 hours per year (assuming you work 48 weeks), or six full workweeks. Tell us you wouldn't like to recapture the equivalent of six extra weeks every year.

How you use that time is limited only by your imagination. You might:

- Develop your knowledge and skills in a new and promising practice area.
- Finally write a series of articles establishing your status as a thought leader in your field and attract more clients.
- Craft a careful plan to grow and scale your business in ways that make it easier to attract a buyer when you're ready to retire.
- Sit on the board of a local business or charity.
- Mentor a junior.
- Become an adjunct professor of law.
- Coach your kid's sports team.
- Practice a hobby.
- Take a real vacation – without checking your inbox every hour...

We've seen this first-hand. When we started working with "Julie", she hadn't taken a holiday with her son in years. Her practice consumed all her time. She worked hard but wasn't as profitable as she should have been because she was doing everything. That changed when she delegated screening and onboarding new clients to an external service, reducing what used to take her 75 minutes multiple times each week, to just 20 minutes each time. She also took on a lawyer to whom she delegated the more routine work in her files. Within the first year of making these changes, Julie was able to afford the time and cost of a one-week vacation with her son. The next year she took a two-week vacation.

The time you get back from delegating isn't just empty space, it's opportunity space. And it multiplies – the more focused your time, the more productive and profitable you become.

There's also a personal side. The time you reclaim gives you the freedom to engage in activities that are important to you and your wellbeing – attending school plays, getting to the gym again, or simply reading a book that isn't about law.

If you want to build a business that supports your life, instead of running it, ask yourself, what's the highest value, best use of your next reclaimed hour?

Where to start – a practical path forward

You won't be able to overhaul your entire practice in a week. It will take some time to take back control of your time, do more of what you love, and be more successful, but you can do it. Here is a simplified action plan you can implement today:

1. *Audit your time.* Write down everything you did yesterday. No detail is too small.
2. *Cross off the things only you could have done.* Be honest. Could someone else have answered that intake call? Proofread your reporting letter? Sent that invoice?
3. *Pick one of the tasks that remains.* Choose just one relatively routine task that currently takes you 30 minutes or so, multiple times a week that you will delegate or automate. We want you to enjoy a real time saving.
4. *Document it.* Use the framework above to create an SOP.
5. *Test and refine your SOP.* You're currently doing the task multiple times a week, so you'll have ample opportunity to test and correct your SOP

before handing it off. The success of your delegation depends on the quality of your SOP.

6. *Hand it off.* Explain the SOP to your delegate, perhaps shadow them while they first implement it, and answer their questions. Then let them execute the process on their own. Provide feedback and further refine the SOP as required.

7. *Invest the time you save.* Invest all the time you save through this initial delegation into creating an SOP for the next task you'll delegate.

If this feels overwhelming, don't worry. The hardest part is getting started. But momentum builds quickly. We've experienced this with clients time and again – one delegated task quickly becomes three, then five, and more. Soon they're building systems that run without their constant involvement and interruptions.

And if you need help building those systems, we can help.[2] You don't have to do this alone, but you *do* have to take the first step – define your Power Zone.

Reclaiming your time, reimagining your practice

Every six minutes you spend on low-value work is six minutes stolen from what matters most – your clients, your business, and your life.

You didn't become a lawyer to chase down unpaid invoices, troubleshoot broken printers, or drown in a sea of unread emails. You became a lawyer to help people solve real problems and to make an impact. But your greatest impact comes when you operate in your Power Zone, doing the work that energizes you – the work you're uniquely qualified to do, the work you love, and the work most aligned with your desire to create real value.

Prioritizing that work and delegating the rest isn't optional anymore. You have limited time, energy, and mental bandwidth. Protect them. Build a business that supports your life instead of one that consumes it.

Every lawyer we work with who commits to working in their Power Zone sees measurable improvements – in revenue, satisfaction, and time. You can too.

You don't need another app or a fancy new system. You need clarity about what matters most and the courage to let go of what doesn't. And if you want help doing that contact us. We'd love to support you.

You don't have to do it all. You just have to do what matters most. Start where you are. Start small. Just start. Now go reclaim your time – build the practice you want and finally have time to enjoy your life!

References

1   Taken from *The Power Zone Playbook for Lawyers*, by Karen Dunn Skinner and David Skinner (2024).

2   https://calendly.com/karen-gimbal/strategy-session

Chapter 3:

Why business development is important and how to make time for it

By Joanna Gaudoin, ClientWise

Time is finite and we all manage it differently. It is very human to make time for the tasks that we both enjoy most and feel best utilize our skills to deliver the strongest rewards.

Some lawyers acknowledge they need to make time for business development, whilst others don't even have it on their radar until it is the cause of pain, such as a barrier to a promotion or an expectation that is challenging to meet, perhaps following a change in role. Ideally, you want to avoid a point of pain!

Why lawyers struggle with business development and how to overcome this

Business development – in other words, bringing in more work – is an area that many lawyers struggle with. There are several reasons behind this:

- Business development is not part of legal training, so it's not seen as a key part of being a lawyer from the outset.
- Not all firms make it part of the role in terms of upskilling people, even at a senior level, never mind a junior one.
- Many lawyers believe their technical expertise alone should be sufficient to bring in new work.
- Lawyers typically like to focus on the legal work itself rather than what they perceive as "selling".
- Traditionally, business development has been seen as the preserve of partners, rather than a focus for all client-facing individuals.
- Many feel they aren't the right "personality fit" for bringing in work.
- Business development time isn't chargeable, and most firms are focused on chargeable hours targets.
- Many lack knowledge regarding what to do.

Many of these barriers can be overcome by focusing on mindset and approach, as follows.

Mindset

It is important to reflect on how much the relationship with a client makes a difference. Legal matters are rarely something that can be "sold" by someone else. In many cases, they are an emotional purchase, even in business-to-business legal services. Ultimately, as a lawyer, you are solving a problem, reducing a risk, or bringing a benefit to the client. Therefore, how you work with clients makes a difference. It isn't a purely transactional piece of work in most cases, even if it is a transaction.

Even if you work for a large, well-known firm, how you engage matters. It might be a cliché, but people buy people.

From the perspective of not wanting to "sell", it is challenging to "sell" a legal service that people don't need. Yes, lawyers can be accused of spending too much time on a matter (which is an issue for another time) but if you are "selling" someone a service they need, then you are helping that client. This positioning can support a shift in how you view business development.

With the right knowledge and skills, combined with your legal expertise, you as a lawyer are the best person to articulate how you can help a prospective client and nurture the relationship so they hopefully become a repeat client or a referral source.

Despite the lack of focus during training, it is essential that lawyers and their firms consider business development at a junior level. Allocating it to partner level only creates many challenges, even dangers, as well as missed opportunities in both the short- and long-term.

Quick wins happen but business development is a marathon, not a sprint, which requires time, consistency, and perseverance.

In the short-term, it may seem a great cost to spend time each week on business development if you equate that to "lost" fees. However, in the medium- to long-term, that can pay back many times over. Imagine you spend six billable hours over a couple of months building a relationship with an accountancy practice. Let's say that is £2,000 of "lost" fees. However, that accountancy practice introduces you to a new client a month from now, which then generates £2,000 in fees per month. The business development time is therefore well worth it!

Approach

Having this clearly set out motivates individuals to focus on it. Available time is scarce and so any time allocated to business development needs to be focused and productive. This is why a clear strategy and plan are essential, otherwise little is likely to happen consistently and when it does, it is likely to be disparate and unfocused activity that doesn't deliver positive outcomes and encourage perseverance.

As an individual, it is essential to consider how you use your personality, skills, and gifts to develop business in a way that works for you. It is not one-size-fits-all – business development plans will vary depending on you as an individual, your area of practice, and your firm. Whilst not everyone will become a significant rainmaker, everyone can improve and contribute to business development.

It is important to have in mind that there are three key levers to generate more work. This will help you be more focused. It might be relevant to focus on all three, or just one or two depending on your practice and situation.

1. *New clients directly*. This is often the most attractive area for individuals as it feels exciting to tell your department that you have a "new" client.

2. *Introducers*. These can be extremely fruitful. These are often other professionals who have clients with a similar profile to you, yet they solve different challenges for them. Making time to build some key introducer relationships can provide you with several new clients a year via one other firm/person. To make this work well, it needs to be strategic and focused on building relationships with those who see the value of this as an activity, regardless of whether you can introduce them to new clients.

3. *Existing clients*. This is often an underdeveloped goldmine. The best part is that these are people you already have a (hopefully positive) relationship with, so there are three key opportunities – to do more similar work for the client, to cross-sell to that client, and finally gain referrals from them to other new clients.

Here are some statistics[1] to substantiate why focusing on existing clients is so vital:

- Acquiring a new client can cost five to 25 times more than retaining an existing one.[2]
- Existing clients spend 67 percent more compared to new clients.[3]
- Eighty-four percent of B2B decision makers begin their buying process with a referral which could come from an existing client.[4]

It pains me to hear of clients using a second law firm for a service the first could have provided. It also puts the work with the first firm at risk, if the second offers the same set of services (many do), builds a better relationship with the client, and offers superior service levels.

The importance of business development for your firm and your career

Gaining new work is the lifeblood of the revenue and profit a firm needs to stay operational, which in turn keeps people employed and helping clients. When there is a focus on growth and this is achieved, the firm can compensate people better, invest in new technology and other resources, and attract and retain the most skilled people. Everybody wins.

Business development is essential for law firms, even if the firm currently seems busy. Whilst many firms have currently got a lot of work and are short of resource, it is interesting to consider how tasks can fill time. If business development is made a priority and each person is required to commit just an hour or two a week (and is being incentivized to do so), you might be surprised how this time could be found.

Markets change and it is easy to fall behind the curve, so having a business development strategy and plan is essential. Think of it like this. If the plumbing system isn't in place, you can't turn the tap on. In legal, there is typically a lower level of repeat work than there is in a profession such as accountancy, so it's vital to have a structured and sustainable approach to bringing in new work.

It is vital to develop the client relationship, so they return to you. This is now more difficult because loyalty is on the decline. Five years ago, most clients would instruct the same firm when they had another need. Now, this is not necessarily the case – anecdotally, only around half return, and the trend is decreasing. It is easier than ever to find a new firm if the service doesn't meet client needs. Therefore, existing client relationships and client development are essential key considerations within your business development strategy.

If there is a structured approach to business development, there is a plan in place to attract other work even if a client is unfortunately "lost".

Another reality is that a lawyer's core role is to win and retain clients. Yes, this is about "what" is delivered but it's also about "how". Legal work doesn't exist in isolation – it is about people. How any lawyer of any level deals with clients has a profound effect on client satisfaction levels. It is often non-partners that have most day-to-day client contact.

Therefore, everyone who is client-facing has a role to play, specifically regarding the "existing clients" lever. It's also worthwhile considering how every individual represents their firm in the wider market and interacts with potential introducers and new clients, even in a personal context.

When a range of lawyers at different levels make time for business development, risk is reduced and opportunities are maximized.

Let's consider the risk element for a moment. Many firms are reliant on a minority of people, usually partners, for bringing in work. What happens if one or some of those people leave or are indisposed?

In terms of opportunity, with more people at different levels contributing to business development, more opportunities will be created and more business brought in. Even relationships built at more junior levels can pay dividends – after all, junior people usually become senior and therefore decision-makers over time.

In career terms, getting involved early will help you stand out positively and actively contribute to your progression. Forward-thinking firms will only promote those who show some commitment to business development (amongst other non-technical skills) to more senior levels. In those firms that do promote on technical ability alone, lawyers can end up finding themselves promoted with a significant expectation around business development and struggle to know where to start. Not getting involved early can also limit you if you wish to move firms.

Making time for business development, whatever your level, is key. If you are already a senior lawyer who is experienced in business development, I would recommend making time to involve your team in business development strategy and planning, as well as upskilling them. Many senior lawyers struggle to explain how they "do" business development. I have heard partners uttering such phrases as, "It's all about the shoe leather" – which is not helpful. If you find this process a challenge, get expert support.

The key building blocks you need to make time for

If you are in a firm that has a structured approach to business development, then it may be a case of plugging into that and looking at how you can support an existing plan or build your own for your practice, as well as upskill as you need to.

If your firm doesn't have a structured approach to business development, depending on the culture, context, and your level, you may want to start a department- or firm-wide initiative yourself. Making some progress before you demonstrate the case for a practice- or firm-wide focus on business development can sometimes be a sensible approach.

My proven framework, *The 5 Ps of Proactive Business Development©*, explains what is needed for business development to be successful. We'll now walk through it so you can evaluate whether you simply have gaps or need to start from the beginning. All of these elements are essential for you to get results from business development, and this section will look at each "P" in brief.

The 5 Ps of Proactive Business Development©

1. Positioning
What this is: Being very clear which services you want to focus on. If someone asked you about the two main ones, what would they be? Also, what sort of clients do you want to focus on? What is the client type you are focusing on for each?

Why this matters: This helps you focus on specific business development activities and helps you be more memorable to others. It doesn't mean you can't offer other services that utilize your expertise, especially when approached by prospective clients, but you need to focus when approaching the market proactively.

How to approach this: To define this, consider which work you are best placed to deliver in terms of expertise and what you enjoy. Where do you get the best results? What type of clients do you seem to attract and who do you most enjoy working with? What is there a market for? Making sure a service is profitable is vital, unless it is an important gateway to bringing in more profitable work.

Being specific helps people remember you. For example, I know one female solicitor who has a passion for helping fathers get a fair divorce settlement with equal child access, so that is what she is known for in the market, rather than a family lawyer who deals with a number of matters. She therefore gets remembered more frequently and is a go-to for clients in that situation.

2. Profile and presence
What this is: Understanding you need your own profile and presence in the market and working on both.

Why this matters: Working for a well-known firm can be valuable but clients assume that pretty much any lawyer has the expertise in their area (sorry!).

Price may be a differentiator but, more often than not, personal recommendation or the impact you have when a prospective client engages with you directly or looks you up online play an important role. The cliché, "people buy people", is true.

How to approach this: Consider the impact you want to have on clients and introducers. What is your "brand"? If people were to describe what you were like to work with, what adjectives would they say that weren't about your legal expertise? What makes you positively memorable? How do you articulate who you help and with what? Lawyers typically solve a current problem, reduce risk, and/or bring a benefit. What do you really help clients with?

3. Prospecting

What this is: Deciding which activities to focus on to generate the work you want with the clients you serve best.

Why this matters: Time is precious and if you haven't thought carefully about which business development activities to focus on, you will end up doing lots of things not very well or nothing at all.

How to approach this: Consider where potential clients and introducers are to be found. Is it at certain events where you could network or even speak? Do they read certain online publications? Consider also the key foundations of where you are represented online and keep these up to date. Potential clients and introducers are likely to consult these to back up what else they know about you. I am particularly thinking about your LinkedIn profile and your firm's website. Reflect on existing clients and how you can develop those relationships further, both during a matter and afterwards, to generate additional opportunities either for your practice area or elsewhere in the firm.

4. People skills

What this is: Making sure you have the skills to build trusted relationships in different professional situations with potential introducers and clients, as well as existing clients. It's also vital to consider internal relationships to generate cross-selling opportunities and to work effectively with your own team to deliver excellence for clients.

Why this matters: Relationships are what make the difference to clients choosing to work with you and work with you more, as well as referrals and of course effective and positive internal working.

How to approach this: Consider the relationships you have and how positive they are. Are there specific situations or types of people that you find more challenging and therefore skills you need to work on? In terms of the prospecting activities you have decided to focus on, reflect on whether you need to develop any specific skills for those, such as public speaking skills or the ability to network positively and confidently to get results.

Making time to work on these skills is an essential part of successful business development. Without people skills, you are not likely to achieve good outcomes. Business development is about assuring prospective clients and introducers that you have the technical skills and credibility and that working with you will be positive and straightforward.

5. Politics
What this is: Politics occurs as people have different values, assumptions, and beliefs.

Why this matters: It can be challenging to understand others and misunderstandings often create political challenges and lead to unhelpful relationship patterns. You might experience this directly internally, which can affect the outcome for clients and whether you build good relationships that encourage cross-selling both ways. However, you may also need to navigate political challenges with clients, particularly if you have corporate clients or clients where multiple family members are involved.

How to approach this: Consider whether you actually know what is really going on or whether you are sometimes quick to jump to conclusions without questioning your assumptions. It's important to consider whether you need a wider network as this can be extremely helpful to build your awareness internally of what goes on. In terms of clients, make sure you always understand who the decision-makers are and try to find out their relative agendas and influence.

Once you have worked through the above and decided what you need to focus on, a final important step is to set yourself some objectives. This will help you know whether you are making progress and, when you review every quarter, decide whether you need to change course.

How to build business development into your working day

Working on *The 5 Ps of Proactive Business Development*© to develop a business development strategy and plan is a pivotal foundational step, so that time spent on business development is sustainable and delivers positive outcomes. It may take you several blocks of time to be clear on your current situation and create a strategy and plan.

Once you have done this, any business development time you plan is likely to be effective and well spent as you will have a specific plan you are working to. To put it simply, it means each time you sit down to do some business development, it will be very clear what you need to focus on.

The vital factor is to block regular time in your diary to execute the plan. If it doesn't become part of business as usual, i.e. a key part of your working life, then it is unlikely you will ever work on business development. If you do, it will be unfocused, sporadic, and unlikely to have positive results, which may lead you to give up entirely.

There will always be seemingly more important or urgent work to do. This will particularly be a challenge if business development is not one of your preferred areas to work on.

Some principles to help you time block:

- Decide how much time per week you want to commit to spend on business development based on your plan and objectives.
- Consider whether you'd prefer one longer block of time or several shorter ones. Experiment with lengths of time to spend on business development. You need long enough to get into some actions but not so long that you become inefficient.
- Select time(s) when you know you can be disciplined and "close the door" on everyone else, either in person or virtually. If you know this is a challenge for you, choose a time of day when you are less likely to be interrupted. Unless executing your plan involves calls and meetings then early in the morning or late at night work well.
- At the end of each week, review progress and ensure you are clear what you will focus on from your plan in your next business development time block.
- Avoid cancelling a slot in your diary unless it is absolutely essential. Once you cancel one slot, it is easy to see it as an optional and disposable space in your diary. If you really have to do something else, move it to another time within the same week, so it still happens.

Another way to use time well that should be considered when you are working on your prospecting activities is to leverage your firm's marketing. How can you build on this from a business development perspective? I would suggest you get to know your firm's marketing person/team so you can understand what is possible. An example is that many marketing departments have an events calendar so you can see what is valuable for you. This will save you time researching events, if networking is one of your designated focus activities.

Once you get into the habit of business development, and dedicate time to it, it will become more normal and much easier. It will also help you spot more opportunities and have other ideas as you go about your everyday work.

How to get the support you need to manage business development effectively

If you are a partner, then making time for business development is going to be expected and accepted. After all, bringing in work and managing client relationships are key responsibilities. My key recommendation for you is to involve your team and develop a business development strategy and plan that brings in different seniority levels of lawyer. It also means business development needs to be embedded into business as usual. Include business development as a regular part of team meetings, discuss it in appraisals, and make it part of compensation consideration. I call this establishing a *business development culture*.

It means more can be achieved as a greater number of individuals are contributing to the plan and different skills can be utilized. It's a valuable concept as not only does it get more done, it involves all levels of lawyer. This means it gets them used to doing business development, so it supports their career progression, as well as growth for the firm. After all, anyone in contact with clients is doing business development – how they interact with them will have a key impact on whether those clients are happy and therefore whether they come back with other work for your firm and/or refer others.

If you are a forward thinking, more junior lawyer wanting to commit to business development, then firstly well done – this puts you ahead of many. However, it could be more challenging to stay committed unless you have partners/other seniors in your team who are themselves focused on business development and believe that a wider range of seniorities need to be involved. It is worth taking the time to consider your experience of business development at your firm – how it is viewed, who is involved. This will then help you move forward more quickly as you will have thought about the context and potential barriers.

Initially, you may be able to work on business development without anyone knowing (not that I would specifically recommend this). However, assuming your plan leads you to doing some business development activities such as networking or meetings such as coffees and lunches that may fall during the day, then this could be challenging.

You will also be likely to need some budget, so this is a point you will need to negotiate. Some activities can be done at limited or no cost but many networking groups have a membership fee, conferences cost money, and you are likely to want to take people for coffee/lunch. It is better if you can negotiate a budget per quarter rather than having to ask every single time otherwise this will slow progress and prevent you from planning well.

This is where the fifth P – *Politics* – in my framework needs careful navigating from an internal point of view. If you know your seniors will be supportive, talk to them early on and discuss your thinking. They will appreciate you involving them and asking for their thoughts. However, if you think your seniors will be less supportive – and there are a variety of reasons why this unfortunately occurs – then my recommendation would be to develop your strategy and plan before you discuss with them what you intend to do (not the detailed plan at this stage) and why. Think about the "why" from their perspective and present the benefits to them and the firm of you doing this.

No firm has a 100 percent chargeable hours target so the first step is to assess how you are currently spending non-chargeable hours and whether you could free some of that time up. That is unlikely to be sufficient though, so you are likely to need to spend additional time. You may therefore have to make the case to redirect a small amount of your chargeable time to business development.

Even if you are not sharing the business development work you are doing, it can be helpful to be accountable to someone and/or have someone you can share ideas with and get input from.

In conclusion

Time is finite and life as a lawyer is busy. However, whatever your career stage as a lawyer in private practice, I hope this chapter has helped you realize that making time for business development is vital. If you are already doing so, what can you do better? Who else can you involve? How can you make time?

My biggest piece of advice is to work through *The 5 Ps of Proactive Business Development©* and put the key foundations in place that will not only give you the key building blocks to develop business but also the plan and momentum you need to make progress. The next step is to block regular time and progress your plan.

So many lawyers and firms are needlessly putting themselves in situations where opportunities are missed. Worse still, they're putting their firms at risk by not having a structured and skilled approach to business development that involves a range of people and is part of business as usual. Business development can sustainably generate additional work over the long-term to maintain the firm's revenue and hopefully grow it.

Remember, business development is a marathon not a sprint – it's all about sustained, well thought-through action. Everyone can move forward with business development, from where they are now.

References

1   Unspecific to the legal market.
2   Harvard Business Review: https://hbr.org/2014/10/the-value-of-keeping-the-right-customers
3   BIA Advisory: www.business.com/articles/returning-customers-spend-67-more-than-new-customers-keep-your-customers-coming-back-with-a-recurring-revenue-sales-model/
4   Worldwide Business Research: www.wbresearch.com/relationship-between-b2b-buying-content-sales-changed-insights.

Chapter 4:
Work–life balance and wellbeing – protecting your health and energy

By Jean-Baptiste Lebelle, HR director, and Alice Boullier de Branche, senior HR manager in the Paris HR team, A&O Shearman

The rise of wellbeing in the legal profession

In the demanding world of business law, time is both a currency and a constraint. The profession's relentless pace, high stakes, and culture of constant availability have long been seen as the (bitter) price of success. Unlike many other professions, the boundaries between professional and personal life are often blurred for lawyers, with urgent matters and client crises frequently intruding into evenings, weekends, and even vacations. Yet, as the legal sector evolves – driven by technological innovation, shifting client expectations, and a growing awareness of mental health – the imperative to manage time effectively has never been more critical. At the heart of this challenge lies the question of work–life balance and wellbeing. Far from being a peripheral concern, the ability to protect one's health and energy is foundational to sustainable performance, professional fulfillment, and long-term career success. Addressing these challenges is essential not only for individual lawyers but also for the profession. By fostering a culture that values wellbeing and supports effective time management, law firms and legal departments can help ensure that their teams remain motivated, engaged, and capable of delivering the highest standard of service without sacrificing their health or personal lives in the process.

The realities and pressures of business law – understanding the landscape

The practice of business law is characterized by a unique blend of intellectual rigor, high expectations, and relentless pace. Lawyers in this field are routinely confronted with intense client demands, the pressure of billable hours, and a professional culture that has long-equated dedication with long hours and constant availability. The advent of digital technology has only intensified these pressures, making it increasingly difficult to draw clear lines between professional and personal life.

The culture of "busyness" in law firms is not merely a byproduct of client demands but is often reinforced by organizational norms and performance metrics. Billable hours remain the dominant measure of productivity and value, incentivizing long working days and discouraging time spent on non-billable activities such as professional development, mentoring, or even rest.

The result is a profession where overwork is normalized, and the boundaries between work and life are increasingly porous. Yet, as recent studies have shown, these realities are not immutable. Recognizing the pressures inherent in business law is the first step toward developing a more sustainable and fulfilling approach to legal practice.

Rethinking work–life balance – a dynamic equilibrium

Work–life balance in the legal profession is frequently misunderstood as a strict division of hours between professional obligations and personal pursuits. In practice, however, it is better understood as a dynamic equilibrium – one that adapts to the evolving demands of both work and life outside the office. For business lawyers, achieving this balance requires flexibility – the ability to respond to client needs while also safeguarding time for family, health, and personal development.

A sustainable approach to balance begins with self-awareness. Lawyers should regularly evaluate their own wellbeing, reflect on their personal limits, and clarify their priorities beyond the workplace. This process of self-assessment enables the setting of realistic boundaries and the making of intentional choices that support both professional achievement and personal fulfilment.

Research underscores the importance of this approach. Professionals who align their schedules with their core values and priorities report higher levels of wellbeing and engagement. Notably, a 2020 study by Whillans et al. introduced the concept of "time affluence" – the sense of having enough time for what matters most – which was found to be a stronger predictor of happiness and life satisfaction than income.[1] Lawyers who make time for personal interests, relationships, and self-care are not only happier but also more effective in their professional roles.

Rather than striving for a perfect split between work and life, the focus should be on establishing a rhythm that accommodates periods of intense professional activity as well as genuine downtime. This rhythm will naturally shift at different stages of a lawyer's career. For example, junior associates may face periods of heavy workload as they build expertise, while senior lawyers often have greater autonomy to shape their schedules. The key is to recognize that balance is not a static goal but a dynamic process requiring ongoing reflection and adjustment.

The reality of legal practice

Historically, work–life balance in law has been viewed as a clear separation between professional and personal time, with the assumption that strict boundaries protect wellbeing. However, the realities of business law – unpredictable client demands, urgent deadlines, and a culture of constant availability – often render this model impractical. The boundaries between work and personal life are frequently blurred, making it difficult to adhere to a fixed schedule or fully disconnect from work. This inflexibility can lead to frustration and a sense of failure when the ideal of perfect balance proves unattainable.

A nuanced approach to time management

In response to these challenges, the concept of "optimal busyness" offers a more adaptive and realistic framework. Rather than seeking a static equilibrium, optimal busyness acknowledges the natural ebb and flow of professional and personal demands. It is defined by a state in which lawyers feel challenged and engaged by their work but not overwhelmed or chronically stressed.

Key elements of optimal busyness include:

- *Dynamic equilibrium.* Optimal busyness is not about maintaining a fixed ratio of work to personal time. It requires continual self-assessment and adjustment. Lawyers should regularly reflect on their wellbeing, reassess priorities, and realign their schedules as circumstances evolve. This flexibility allows for periods of intense focus, balanced by genuine opportunities for rest and renewal.
- *Intentional alignment.* Rather than focusing solely on separation, optimal busyness emphasizes aligning work with personal values and priorities. Lawyers are encouraged to clarify what matters most to them and to make conscious choices that support these priorities. This may involve accepting periods of high workload when they serve meaningful goals, while also ensuring that time is protected for family, health, and personal growth.
- *Challenged, not overwhelmed.* The aim is to achieve a level of busyness that is stimulating and productive, without tipping into excess.

Research shows that professionals are most satisfied when they experience enough organizational control to feel challenged, but not so much that they become fatigued or burnt out. This state is associated with energy, focus, and a sense of progress, rather than exhaustion and disengagement.

- *Ongoing reflection and adjustment.* Unlike traditional models, optimal busyness requires proactive recognition of the signs of excessive busyness – such as persistent exhaustion, irritability, or difficulty disconnecting from work – and taking corrective action. This may involve setting firmer boundaries, delegating tasks, or seeking support from colleagues and mentors.
- *Shared responsibility.* Achieving optimal busyness is not solely an individual task. Law firms and legal departments play a crucial role by fostering a culture that values reasonable working hours, supports flexible arrangements, and provides access to wellbeing resources. Leadership must model healthy behaviors and support team members in managing workloads, ensuring that the pursuit of optimal busyness is sustainable for all.

Risks and opportunities of optimal busyness

While optimal busyness offers a promising alternative to rigid work–life balance models, it is not without risks. Research by Lupu and Rokka highlights that professionals may become addicted to the feeling of being busy, prioritizing short-term productivity at the expense of long-term wellbeing.[2] This can lead to cycles of overwork and burnout, as individuals chase the elusive sense of being "in the zone".

To avoid these pitfalls, lawyers must learn to recognize the signs of excessive busyness and take proactive steps to restore balance. This may involve setting boundaries, prioritizing rest, and seeking support from colleagues and mentors. Organizations, for their part, must be mindful of the impact of their expectations and controls on employee wellbeing, striving to create conditions that support optimal busyness without tipping into excess.

Optimal busyness represents a departure from traditional, rigid models of work–life balance, embracing a more flexible, responsive, and holistic approach. It recognizes that the realities of legal practice demand adaptability, self-awareness, and ongoing adjustment. By seeking a state where challenge and control are balanced, lawyers can maintain high performance and professional fulfilment without sacrificing their health or personal lives.

This dynamic model is better suited to the complexities of modern legal work and is essential for long-term wellbeing and career sustainability in the profession.

The consequences and benefits of balance – scientific insights

Neglecting work–life balance carries well-documented risks, including burnout, anxiety, depression, and a host of physical health issues. The legal profession in particular has been identified in studies by the American Bar Association as having higher rates of mental health challenges compared to other fields due to the profession's high expectations, constant client demands, and the culture of long working hours.[3] Common warning signs of imbalance include persistent exhaustion, difficulty concentrating, irritability, sleep disturbances, and a sense of detachment from both work and personal relationships.[4] For example, a lawyer who finds themselves regularly missing family events, feeling unable to disconnect from work emails, or experiencing frequent headaches and insomnia may be exhibiting early symptoms of burnout. Recognizing these signals early is crucial for taking corrective action before more serious health consequences develop.[5] Chronic stress not only undermines personal wellbeing but also erodes professional effectiveness, leading to reduced productivity, increased errors, and strained relationships.

A 2016 study by Krill, Johnson, and Albert found that 28 percent of lawyers suffered from depression, 19 percent from anxiety, and 21 percent from problematic drinking.[6] These figures are significantly higher than those found in the general population and underscore the urgent need for systemic change in the profession. The study also found that the primary drivers of these outcomes were excessive workload, lack of control over work schedules, and the expectation of constant availability.

Conversely, lawyers who maintain a healthy balance enjoy improved mental and physical health, greater job satisfaction, and enhanced creativity. They are also more likely to sustain long and rewarding careers. These findings are echoed in longitudinal studies, such as those published in *The Lancet Psychiatry*, which demonstrate that regular rest, social connection, and self-care are protective factors against professional burnout.[7]

The benefits of balance extend beyond individual wellbeing to organizational performance. Firms that support work–life balance report lower turnover, higher employee engagement, and better client outcomes. A 2019 study by the University of Oxford's Saïd Business School found that happy employees are 13 percent more productive, a finding that holds true in the legal sector as well.[8] By investing in the wellbeing of their lawyers, firms can enhance both their reputation and their bottom line.

Strategies for sustainable practice – individual and organizational approaches

Achieving and maintaining work–life balance in business law requires a blend of personal strategies and supportive organizational practices. Effective time management is not merely a matter of productivity – it is fundamental to sustaining mental health and overall wellbeing. Increasingly, business lawyers are recognizing the necessity of approaching their schedules with intention, ensuring that professional obligations are balanced with personal values and priorities. This involves a conscious effort to set clear boundaries around work hours, thereby avoiding the common pitfall of overextension that can lead to burnout.

Structuring the working day

Allocating specific periods for focused work, client meetings, and administrative responsibilities enables lawyers to establish a structured routine that supports both efficiency and personal fulfilment. Regularly reviewing and adjusting these schedules is essential to maintaining a healthy equilibrium between professional and personal life. Establishing and communicating boundaries is particularly important in the digital age, where the expectation of constant availability can be overwhelming. Lawyers should make deliberate choices to limit after-hours emails and calls, using out-of-office notifications when necessary to signal unavailability. Designating technology-free times throughout the day allows for meaningful disconnection and recharging, and it is equally important to encourage clients and colleagues to respect these boundaries. Such practices not only protect personal time but also foster a culture of mutual respect within the professional environment.

Leveraging technology wisely

The strategic use of technology can greatly enhance efficiency, but it must be approached with discernment to avoid technostress. Automating routine and repetitive tasks, such as document management and scheduling, can free up valuable time for more complex legal work. However, it is important to regularly evaluate the effectiveness of digital tools and eliminate those that contribute to stress or distraction. Taking regular breaks from screens is also vital to reduce fatigue and maintain focus throughout the workday.

Prioritizing self-care

Prioritizing self-care is a fundamental aspect of sustainable legal practice. Incorporating regular exercise, even in the form of brief walks during the day, can have a significant positive impact on both physical and mental health. Making conscious choices about nutrition, such as opting for balanced meals and staying adequately hydrated, supports sustained energy and cognitive function. Above all, prioritizing sufficient sleep is essential, as it underpins emotional resilience and the ability to perform at a high level. A 2018 meta-analysis published in *Sleep* found that sleep deprivation impairs cognitive performance, decision-making, and emotional regulation – all critical skills for lawyers.[9] Similarly, regular physical activity has been shown to reduce stress, improve mood, and enhance resilience.

Creating a productive work environment

For lawyers operating in remote or hybrid settings, the importance of a well-structured and productive work environment cannot be overstated. The physical separation of work and personal spaces is a fundamental principle that underpins effective time management and overall professional success. By establishing a dedicated workspace, legal professionals can foster an atmosphere that is conducive to concentration, efficiency, and wellbeing.

A dedicated workspace should be organized, comfortable, and intentionally designed to minimize distractions. This means selecting a location within the home or office that is quiet and removed from high-traffic areas, ensuring that interruptions from family members, housemates, or external noise are kept to a minimum.

Comfort is another essential consideration. Ergonomic furniture, such as an adjustable chair and desk, can help prevent physical discomfort and long-term health issues associated with prolonged periods of sitting. Adequate lighting, preferably natural light, can improve mood and alertness, while personal touches – such as artwork or plants – can make the space more inviting and pleasant.

Minimizing distractions is critical for maintaining focus. This may involve setting boundaries with others in the household, using noise-cancelling headphones, or employing digital tools to block distracting websites and notifications during work hours. Establishing clear routines and work schedules can further reinforce the separation between professional and personal time, helping lawyers to mentally transition between roles and maintain a healthy work–life balance.

Building support networks

The legal profession can sometimes be isolating, making it important for lawyers to actively build and maintain support networks. Fostering relationships with colleagues, seeking mentorship, and offering support to peers all contribute to a sense of community and shared purpose. Participation in professional associations and networking events can further broaden these support systems, providing valuable opportunities for connection and collaboration.

Managing expectations and workload

Managing client expectations through transparent communication and the judicious use of the word "no" is a critical skill, allowing lawyers to protect the quality of their work and their own wellbeing. This is not about shirking responsibility but about setting realistic expectations and ensuring that commitments can be met without compromising health or quality. By protecting personal time and learning to decline non-essential tasks or meetings, lawyers not only safeguard their wellbeing but also enhance their professional effectiveness, delivering higher quality work and maintaining long-term motivation. Research by Leslie Perlow at Harvard Business School has shown that teams that collectively agree to "predictable time off" not only experience less burnout but also deliver better results for clients.[10]

Prioritizing tasks, delegating effectively, and leveraging technology to automate routine work can help manage overwhelming caseloads. The 80/20 rule – focusing on the tasks that deliver the greatest value – can be a powerful tool for maximizing impact while minimizing unnecessary effort. Delegation is equally important, both as a means of managing workload and as an opportunity for junior lawyers to develop their skills.

The role of organizations

At the organizational level, law firms play a crucial role in shaping the conditions for work–life balance. Firms that promote a culture of reasonable working hours, value outcomes over presenteeism, and provide access to wellbeing resources create an environment where lawyers can thrive. Flexible working arrangements, such as remote work and adaptable schedules, have been shown in research from the University of Oxford to improve both productivity and wellbeing when implemented thoughtfully.[11]

Leadership is essential in modelling healthy behaviors and supporting team members in setting boundaries. Training in time management, resilience, and stress management can further equip lawyers to navigate the demands of their roles. Ultimately, fostering a culture that prioritizes wellbeing is not only beneficial for individuals but also enhances the reputation and sustainability of the profession as a whole.

The collective responsibility – culture, leadership, and the profession

The challenge of achieving genuine work–life balance in the legal profession is not merely an individual concern – it is a collective responsibility that demands a fundamental shift in culture, leadership, and professional norms. While personal strategies are important, it is the broader environment – shaped by law firm policies, leadership attitudes, and industry expectations – that ultimately determines whether lawyers can truly thrive.

Transforming culture and policy

Firms that are serious about change are moving beyond token gestures. They are embedding policies that prioritize reasonable working hours, reward outcomes rather than mere presence, and provide robust access to mental health and wellbeing resources. These firms recognize that a healthy workforce is not only more productive but also more innovative and resilient. Flexible working is no longer a privilege but a standard expectation, and firms that fail to adapt risk losing talent to more progressive competitors.

The role of leadership

Leadership is pivotal in driving this transformation. Leaders must model healthy behaviors, openly discuss their own boundaries, and actively support team members in managing workloads. The tone set at the top cascades throughout the organization. Investment in training – covering time management, resilience, and stress management – equips lawyers at all levels to navigate the profession's demands. Moreover, leaders must foster an environment where open conversations about workload, stress, and mental health are not only accepted but encouraged. This openness helps to dismantle the stigma around seeking help and normalizes the challenges that many lawyers face.

Collective action and support networks

Collective responsibility means that every member of the firm, from senior partners to trainees, has a role to play in building a supportive environment. Peer support networks, mentoring programs, and regular check-ins can provide invaluable guidance and emotional support, particularly for junior lawyers and those new to the profession. By encouraging collaboration and mutual support, firms can create a sense of belonging and shared purpose that strengthens both individual and organizational resilience.

A sustainable future for the profession

Ultimately, prioritizing wellbeing is not just a moral imperative – it is essential for the long-term sustainability and reputation of the legal profession. By embracing collective responsibility, transforming culture, and championing inclusive leadership, the legal sector can create an environment where all lawyers are empowered to succeed, both professionally and personally. The time for change is now, and the firms that lead the way will set the standard for the future of the profession.

Thriving in business law through sustainable time management

Work–life balance and wellbeing are not peripheral concerns for business lawyers – they are foundational to sustained excellence and fulfillment in the profession. By understanding the unique pressures of legal practice, embracing a dynamic approach to balance, and leveraging both personal and organizational strategies, lawyers can protect their health and energy while delivering exceptional service to their clients.

The integration of technology, when approached thoughtfully, can further support these goals, enabling lawyers to focus on the work that matters most. As the profession continues to evolve, a collective commitment to wellbeing will ensure that lawyers not only survive but truly thrive in their careers.

The pursuit of optimal busyness – where challenge and control are balanced, and time is managed with intention – offers a compelling vision for the future of business law. By prioritizing wellbeing, embracing innovation, and fostering a supportive professional culture, lawyers can reclaim their time, enhance their performance, and build careers that are both successful and sustainable.

References

1   Whillans, A. V., Weidman, A. C. and Dunn, E. W. (2020). "Valuing time over money is associated with greater social connection." *Harvard Business Review*, January 2020.

2   Lupu, I. and Rokka, J. (2021). "Busy and Engaged: The Relationship Between Busyness and Well-Being in the Workplace." *Harvard Business Review*, July 2021.

3   American Bar Association, National Task Force on Lawyer Well-Being (2017). "The Path to Lawyer Well-Being: Practical Recommendations for Positive Change."

4   Krill, P. R., Johnson, R. and Albert, L. (2016). "The Prevalence of Substance Use and Other Mental Health Concerns Among American Attorneys." *Journal of Addiction Medicine*.

5   Harvey, S. B., Modini, M., Joyce, S., Milligan-Saville, J. S., Tan, L., Mykletun, A. and Mitchell, P. B. (2017). "Can work make you mentally ill? A systematic meta-review of work-related risk factors for common mental health problems." *The Lancet Psychiatry.*

6   Oswald, A. J., Proto, E. and Sgroi, D. (2015). "Happiness and Productivity." *Journal of Labor Economics.*

7   Sharma, A., Madaan, V. and Petty, F. D. (2006). "Exercise for mental health." *Primary Care Companion to The Journal of Clinical Psychiatry.*

8   Koch, R. (1998). "The 80/20 Principle: The Secret to Achieving More with Less." Crown Business.

9   Lowe, C. J., Safati, A. and Hall, P. A. (2017). "The neurocognitive consequences of sleep restriction: A meta-analytic review." *Sleep Medicine Reviews.*

10 Mazmanian, M., Orlikowski, W. J. and Yates, J. (2013). "The Autonomy Paradox: The Implications of Mobile Email Devices for Knowledge Professionals." *Organization Science.*

11 Bloom, N., Liang, J., Roberts, J. and Ying, Z. J. (2015). "Does working from home work? Evidence from a Chinese experiment." *The Quarterly Journal of Economics.*

Chapter 5:
The impact of working from home – efficiency or distraction?

By Nikki Alderson, international talent retention and women's leadership specialist, TEDx speaker, coach, author, and former criminal barrister

A profession transformed

In early 2020, the legal profession underwent a transformation it had long resisted. Almost overnight, due to the global COVID-19 pandemic, the rigid, office-based, courtroom-bound, lives of lawyers shifted to remote working. Kitchen tables replaced boardrooms. Cloakroom cupboards masqueraded as Chambers, certainly in the case of one barrister client of mine. Video calls replaced court appearances and client meetings. In the UK, "CVP" (or Cloud Video Platform) and *"You're on mute..."* became daily utterances, whilst Zoom took its position as a household name.

For years previously, flexibility was treated by many legal organizations as an unhelpful indulgence, dangerous even, the prevailing wisdom being that productivity came only with visibility – and presenteeism equated to performance. Lawyers were expected to demonstrate commitment through long hours and physical attendance. But when the world shut down, suddenly, the unthinkable became reality – firms transitioned overnight to remote operations.

As the world turned on a sixpence, "working from home" (WFH) became less a novelty, more a necessity. The COVID-19 pandemic represented the ultimate and arguably most radical catalyst for a profession steeped in tradition to rethink its ways of working – do or die.

Unexpectedly, far from chaos, something extraordinary happened – productivity not only held firm but, in certain cases, increased. Perhaps no surprise to those already in the know – one survey on remote working productivity from five years prior[1] found that 77 percent of remote workers said they were *more* productive whilst working from home, whilst 24 percent stated they did *more work in the same time*, and 30 percent said they did *more work in less time.*

The experiment nobody wanted had proven one thing beyond reasonable doubt – the legal world certainly did not implode whilst lawyers worked from home. For many in law, this shift was revolutionary. Practices that had once resisted flexibility were forced to reckon with a new way of working – one that exposed outdated assumptions and opened the door to broader inclusion and efficiency.

As the dust settles in this post-pandemic landscape, the legal world continues to grapple with a critical question concerning the COVID-19 legacy – has remote work improved productivity, performance, and efficiency, or has it eroded focus, increased the risk of distraction and isolation, and blurred boundaries to the point of burnout?

This chapter explores both sides of this debate, specifically through the lens of the legal profession, considering the realities of remote, home working and, most importantly, offers concrete strategies, for individuals, leaders, and teams, to make the most of working remotely in a home-based work environment, without succumbing to the pitfalls.

The pros of remote work for lawyers

Increased productivity and flexibility

Numerous studies from the pandemic period revealed a surprising trend – productivity didn't collapse under remote conditions, indeed in some cases, it soared. According to a Thomson Reuters Report, global law firms managed to boost productivity in the pandemic year, achieving a 12.2 percent increase in hours worked.[2]

Freed from commutes, office noise, and frequent interruptions, lawyers discovered the power of quiet, concentrated work. Legal professionals, already adept at self discipline, found they could better manage their schedules and deliver high-quality work on their own terms.

Autonomy and wellbeing

Autonomy is closely linked to job satisfaction and positive mental health. The pandemic shift granted lawyers greater flexibility and less judgment around their ways of working. Indeed, research from the European Commission's Social Situation Monitor, analyzing data from France, Germany, the UK, and Italy found that in all but the latter country, people working from home reported slightly higher levels of wellbeing on average.[3] To this day, working from home empowers lawyers to tailor their work life for maximum output and personal wellbeing. That autonomy can contribute to reduced stress and a greater sense of control, both protective factors against burnout.

Inclusivity and talent retention

Remote work has been especially impactful for female lawyers and care-givers, who often shoulder disproportionate domestic responsibilities. For many, working from home meant the ability to stay in the profession during periods when rigid office hours might have forced them out.

Flexible work remains a cornerstone for talent retention. Post-pandemic, many women, including many of my current coaching clients, returning from career breaks, cite remote and hybrid working as non-negotiable. It enables continuity in career progression without sacrificing caring respon-sibilities or commuting hours – allowing them to define success on their own terms, as opposed to trying to uncomfortably shoehorn into a traditional (arguably outdated) hierarchical business model.

Inclusivity also extended beyond gender. Lawyers with physical or mental health conditions, and other caring responsibilities, found that flexible home working created opportunities that would otherwise have remained unavail-able.

A post-COVID cultural reboot

"The Great Resignation" signaled a wider cultural reckoning in the workplace, particularly in the US, with many citing the search for better work–life balance as their motivation. In the UK, too, resignations hit a 20-year high.[4]

The pandemic forced a long-overdue rethink of what a lawyer's life could – and should – look like too. Solicitors and barristers, often subject to relentless pressure and long hours, began questioning the culture of "busyness" as a badge of honor. Remote working offered an opportunity to rewrite the rules.

Law firms embracing flexible and hybrid models are now well-positioned to attract and retain talent, particularly among Gen Z and Millennials prior-itizing wellbeing and purposeful work.

The cons and controversies of remote work

High-profile pushback

Despite many clear benefits, remote work has had its high profile and vocif-erous critics. David Solomon, CEO of Goldman Sachs, famously called remote work an *"aberration"* to be corrected by a swift return of employees to the office. Lord Alan Sugar derided home workers as *"lazy layabouts"* while former M&S and ASDA CEO, Stuart Rose, claimed working from home meant an entire generation is *"not doing proper work"*.

In law, similar sentiments exist. Some senior partners fear the erosion of firm culture, mentoring, and client rapport. For traditionalists, being physically present still equates to being productive, and has been reflected in the recent recall of employees by many US law firms to the office for a mandated minimum of four days a week.[5]

Detrimental impact on visibility, team culture, and training

Some concerns held weight during the pandemic. For trainees and junior lawyers especially, the lack of informal learning proved challenging. The pandemic saw many confined to working in shared accommodation or cramped, unsuitable spaces, missing out on learning by osmosis – those insights usually gained by observing more experienced colleagues in action. Mentoring coffee chats with senior leaders, casual "water cooler" moments with contemporaries, and spontaneous collaboration with team members, all felt harder to replicate online. Yet these are the things often considered integral to building relationships, igniting "lightbulbs" and playing an essential role in career progression and workplace cohesion.

Remote work continues to present similar challenges, intensifying feelings of loneliness for those pre-disposed to it, particularly so for those living alone or new to the profession. Without daily human interaction, lawyers may feel isolated or invisible. Visibility is often credited as being a necessary requirement for promotional success. Lawyers who ordinarily feel confident, sharing ideas or concerns in real life, may yet hesitate via email or Zoom, creating further obstacles to advancement.

Without intentional effort, there is a danger that teams become fragmented too, as more people work from home, on increasing numbers of days per week, leaving less experienced lawyers in particular feeling disconnected and unsupported.

Distraction dilemmas – digital and domestic

The most obvious pandemic irony was that technology, while indispensable to keep everyone working and connected, brought with it a major downside – the *"always on"* expectation. With laptops permanently open and phones constantly buzzing, the temptation (and pressure) to respond instantly to emails, even when sent late at night, became habitual. A concerning culture of digital presenteeism emerged and still pervades today – if not visible in the office, there can be a sense that you have to prove your value by being available online, at all times.

Digital distraction continues to pose a significant threat to deep, focused work, whether working remotely or indeed in the office, although arguably heightens at home. Lawyers, often praised for their attention to detail and analytical rigor, find themselves checking inboxes on numerous devices, multiple times a day, switching between tasks and losing focus. This fragmented attention costs us dear considering the time it takes to resume the same level of concentration up to the point of distraction – according to a University of California Irvine study, an average of 23 minutes and 25 seconds.[6] A most extreme example came in the form of a senior barrister client dealing with what she described as a "WhatsApp addiction", exaggerated whilst working from home, and which she was overcoming only with assistance from a Chambers colleague locking her phone away during the day.

When it comes to working remotely, not all home environments are conducive to deep, contemplative work. Lawyers juggling busy households and caring responsibilities may struggle to focus on complex legal tasks. The temptation to multitask or drift into non-work activities can be high without the structure of an office or working in Chambers, causing productivity depletion and decision fatigue whilst constantly wearing, and switching between, different hats.

Burnout and blurred boundaries

Whilst working from home, without careful boundary-setting, there's a risk that work bleeds into personal lives, increasing the risk of burnout. I saw it countless times through the pandemic, particularly with female family lawyer clients, when homes became offices, compromising and blurring the lines between work, family time, and rest. For barristers, court and tribunal hearings moved online to the CVP. While this offered convenience, it also meant an insidious "workload creep" that caught many by surprise.

Despite the disappearance of the daily commute, longer workdays took hold. The remote court working day started earlier, finished later, and was more full-on than ever before, with relentless, back-to-back hearings, longer CVP court hours and available cases, together with the inevitable extended screen time. Many lawyers found themselves sitting in virtual courtrooms with minimal breaks, the working day having expanded to fill all available time.

One of those family law barrister clients put it simply: *"I'm no longer working from home. I'm living at work."* She wasn't alone experiencing the surge in burnout. According to a 2021 Indeed survey, reported by Forbes, over 52 percent of workers said they experienced burnout – an increase of nine percent from the previous year.[7] Lawyers were no exception. Long hours, emotionally intense cases, and high expectations – all amplified by isolation – led to increased stress, anxiety, and exhaustion. According to LawCare's *Life in the Law* report, lawyer respondents exhibited high burnout risk, 69 percent of whom reported experiencing mental ill health in that first pandemic year.[8]

Cultivating focus and productivity, connection and longevity – practical strategies for leaders, individuals, and teams

Having explored some of the possible consequences of remote work, now it's time to turn to solutions. How can we preserve the benefits of working from home – flexibility, accessibility, increased inclusion – while actively addressing the downsides of distraction, disconnection, and burnout?

The answer lies in creating clear healthy boundaries and building positive working cultures – not just at the individual level, but within teams and across leadership.

Below are strategies grouped for three audiences – leaders, individuals, and teams.

Leadership responsibilities in a remote-first culture

In law, leadership often sets the tone for everyone else. Partners, heads of chambers, and senior leaders have a critical role to play in shaping expectations around balance, boundaries, and wellbeing. Leadership in a remote world also requires intention, adaptability, and trust.

Model healthy behaviors

Leaders must support remote working lawyers in setting clear limits. Lead by example. Model the kind of behavior you want to see. Don't simply issue wellbeing memos, live by them – taking the firm wellness days too! True leadership lies in walking the talk and normalizing healthy practices.

Set clear digital boundaries, for example:

- Log off on time.
- Consider using delayed email delivery, where appropriate, to avoid sending messages outside traditional 9-5 working hours.
- Set and communicate firm guidelines for digital availability, such as:
    - *"No Teams messages after 6pm unless urgent."*
    - *"Emails will be answered within 24 hours, not instantly."*

    This manages expectation and reduces or minimizes the *"always on"* pressure.

Encourage focused and deep work. Support time-blocking and non-interruptive workflows. Encourage colleagues to turn off notifications during focus periods and use Out of Office settings during concentrated work blocks. Minimize meetings where possible.

Promote a shared purpose by encouraging feedback and career planning conversations
Help your team connect virtually with the wider vision. This sense of shared meaning builds motivation and cohesion – even when everyone is working in different physical spaces.

Recognize and reward remote achievements and virtual contributions
In remote set-ups, hard work can go unseen. Leaders must actively recognize contributions – verbally, in writing, or during meetings. A well-timed "thank you" can sustain motivation and morale.

Value outcomes over hours. Rather than measuring performance by how many hours are clocked, focus on the quality and impact of work. This allows more flexibility for individuals working from home to find their most productive routines.

Foster openness, encourage collaboration, and create a culture of psychological safety
Encourage honest conversations, even remotely. Make it acceptable – better still, easy – online to ask for help or admit when someone is overloaded. Those working from home, in particular junior team members, should feel comfortable saying, virtually, *"I don't have capacity".*

Prioritize remote check-ins, mentoring, even social events, to aid inclusion. Short, informal calls are still effective to foster connection and reinforce belonging.

Strategies for individuals to thrive when working from home
Ultimately, each legal professional must take responsibility for maintaining their wellbeing and productivity whilst working from home. This involves making conscious choices to shape your work life, rather than letting it shape you.

Set clear and healthy boundaries
- Establish a designated workspace, even if it's small, for optimum focus and productivity.

- Define your working hours and communicate them positively. People far prefer hearing a list of all the things you *will* do, and when, rather than a long list of all the things you won't.
- Occasionally, this may mean learning to say no. Appreciate that not every opportunity or task serves your goals. Pause before accepting new responsibilities. Ask yourself:
  - Does this help my career development?
  - Does it align with my wellbeing?
  - Do I realistically have the time?
  If not, respond professionally but firmly – perhaps with a "not now" or a re-direction to a teammate. Soft boundaries are still boundaries.
- Use rituals to mark the start and end of your day. For example, a morning walk can mentally replace the daily commute. An evening "logging off" or "shutdown" routine can help draw a line under, and clearly signify the end of, the working day.

Reframe productivity
- Don't mistake constant activity for effectiveness. To ensure you stay productive, set daily goals and reflect on progress. Take pride in your outcomes, as opposed to the "busyness".
- Avoid digital presenteeism, or overcompensating to "prove" you're working.

Approach the working day intentionally
- Prepare your week in advance.
- Start the day with a clear plan, prioritizing critical tasks.
- Use time-blocking for deep-focused legal work / research / drafting.
- Use the flexibility of working from home to create routines that support your energy levels. For example, take regular breaks to maintain mental clarity and protected personal time.

Use technology wisely
- Silence unhelpful and distracting digital noise by limiting unnecessary notifications.
- Use inbox batching – by checking emails at designated times throughout the day.
- Activate airplane mode during focus sessions.
- Keep separate devices for work and personal life, where possible.
- Be intentional about camera use in meetings.

Prioritize wellbeing and burnout prevention
- Maintain a healthy routine. Prioritize movement, hydration, and sleep.
- Take wellbeing days where available / needed.
- Create space for non-work conversation with colleagues.
- Be kind to yourself on unproductive days – they happen to everyone.
- Proactively seek remote support. Whether through coaching, mentorship, or peer discussion, talking about challenges, even virtually, builds resilience. If you're struggling, speak up – sooner rather than later. Getting help is a sign of strength, not weakness.

Teams – building boundaries together

Even the most resilient individuals struggle in teams working from home without shared norms or mutual respect. Team cohesion becomes essential in a remote environment.

Clearly define expectations
Agree as a team:
- What are the working hours?
- When are responses expected?
- What is the protocol for urgent matters?

Agree on communication norms
Use an agreed platform, such as Microsoft Teams, Google Chat, Slack, Discord, or email, through which to communicate, collaborate, and share as a team, whilst being clear about preferred methods and times. Make it acceptable to delay email replies until normal working hours. Schedule messages to avoid late-night pings. Set "Do Not Disturb" hours to protect deep work, communicated across the whole team.

Share the load
Encourage fair work distribution. If one team member can't take on more, another might. But this must be reciprocal and trust-based. Regular, honest, virtual communication about capacity is essential.

Celebrate the wins and the people
Recognition should be regular in the remote working environment. Call out good work, team spirit, and effort. Consider virtual weekly team shout-outs or rotating roles to lead meetings. Recognition connects people to purpose and promotes confidence around visibility too.

Home working as a cultural catalyst

A shift in thinking – work–life balance or work–life blend?

The reality for modern professionals – particularly those working remotely – is that work and life are no longer neatly separated. The binary phrase "work–life balance" (suggesting two competing forces, constantly in tension – work on one side, life on the other) is outdated. Instead, lawyers successfully working from home have become accustomed to expertly embrace "work–life integration" or "work–life blend". Work calls happen in kitchens. Legal contracts are amended and skeleton submissions perfected at dining tables. Parenting duties and client meetings collide, in ways never imagined pre-2020.

Rather than resist this, more open-minded legal professionals are adapting, and adopting a growth mindset, by asking:

- What does balance mean for me?
- What approach makes me most productive and present?
- What boundaries will allow me to function optimally, and on purpose?

Each answer is personal. And critically, each one can be supported – even enhanced – by the flexibility offered by remote working, when managed with care and intention.

The hidden drivers – trust and retention

Let's not lose sight of the business case. Burnout and poor work–life balance / blend drive people away. The legal profession is already seeing the consequences – resignations, relocations, and shifting aspirations. Seemingly, the best talent is no longer prepared to sacrifice personal wellbeing for professional status. Look no further than the hugely inflated newly qualified salaries to see how certain firms are attempting to incentivize a literal, as well as figurative, "pay off" – US firms with offices in the UK to the tune of around £175,000; Magic Circle firms at around £150,000.[9]

If firms want to retain talent – especially mid-career women, parents, and diverse candidates – flexibility is what's non-negotiable, not the £100k+ financials. It must be combined with:

- Visible leadership.
- Open dialogue.
- Cultural safety.
- Clear boundaries.
- A "healthy dose of hybrid" – a *combination* of both home and office work availability, to suit individual needs.

Trust is the foundation. Loyalty is engendered. Lawyers trusted to deliver work on their terms often go above and beyond. When they are not, they become disengaged and can walk away altogether.

Sustainable benefits of working from home

Flexible working, including working from home, is here to stay. Hybrid working – a combination of both office and home-based work – is what people want and, indeed more recently, are demanding from their current and new roles. That's supported by a 2024 Recruiter Survey, where over 40 percent of trainee solicitors voted *flexibility* as the top priority when searching for an NQ role.[10]

The debate about working from home needn't fixate on geography – "office vs home". It is more about culture, trust, and choice. Remote working is neither a panacea nor the end of collaboration. It is a tool that, when used well, and in a creative combination of ways, enhances productivity, promotes inclusion, and protects wellbeing.

The legal profession is at a crossroads. The pandemic showed us the road to a more flexible, inclusive, and human-centered way of working, making working from home possible within law. But we are still learning to navigate walking along it, thoughtfully, confidently – and together.

For law firms, the choice is clear. Adapt to offer working from home in a meaningful way or risk becoming irrelevant in the eyes of the modern workforce. Countless times we see evolving law firms thrive, whilst those clinging to old norms risk fading into obscurity, to suffer fates like Blockbuster videos and Kodak films, so many moons ago.

To succeed, leaders must model healthy boundaries, show empathy, and design systems that serve real human needs. For senior leaders, virtual leadership is simply different, not less.

For lawyers, particularly women, and those returning from career breaks, remote working represents not compromise, but opportunity – to define success, achieve balance, and progress careers, on their own terms. Such individuals must be proactive in protecting their focus, confidence, and energy.

Teams must communicate openly and define their "new normal", accommodating home workers collectively.

The result? Happier, healthier professionals. Increased trust and loyalty. Improved retention. Greater diversity. And a far more modern profession.

Whether working from home becomes a source of efficiency or distraction ultimately depends on how we lead, support, and empower people within this new, blended, hybrid way of working. With the right mindset, structures, and support, it can clearly be both efficient and empowering.

Case study: A tale of two lawyers

Let's consider two real-world scenarios,* drawn from lawyer coaching clients over recent years.

Anya – thriving after maternity leave

Anya, a senior associate, promoted whilst on maternity leave, credits working remotely with enhancing both her career and family life.

Prior to the birth of her second child, she and her husband sold up and moved for a different "life in the country", from the big city where her firm was based, to the Lake District.

Before taking maternity leave, she negotiated a hybrid working arrangement that allowed her to prepare cases, meet deadlines, and attend client calls all from home, without sacrificing school runs or risking burnout with prohibitively lengthy daily commutes. Had she not been able to find a way to make it work, she would have left the profession.

Her job satisfaction rose immeasurably, as did the loyalty she felt towards her firm for being so innovative, flexible, and accommodating around home working. Anya's brilliant legal mind and talent were therefore retained – not only within law, but specifically within her existing law firm too.

Within a few short years, predominantly working from home, she was promoted to legal director.

Hannah – burnout and resignation

In contrast, Hannah, a senior criminal barrister with 16 years' experience, was unable to practice from home (or indeed in any way part-time) due to the nature of Crown Court sitting hours and expectations of the serious, back-to-back jury trials in which she ordinarily appeared.

With two children under the age of three, no other flexible or affordable childcare available, and having attempted a return to practice which on a number of occasions had left her compromised (for example, when judges asked to sit longer than usual court hours, either early or late, jeopardizing nursery drop off or collection), she was left with no choice.

Hannah resigned – a sad, yet avoidable, loss to the Bar, had her return been better managed with creative forward-planning and robust support from Chambers and clerks. She now works fully remotely, successfully running a home-based business.

The experiences of Anya and Hannah highlight the real challenges around the need within the legal profession for flexible, home-based working opportunities. Working from home isn't for everyone, nor indeed is it *available* to everyone (as Hannah's case demonstrates). And there's certainly no "one-size-fits-all". But with the right support, remote working is undeniably a powerful force for good in law.

All names changed to preserve anonymity and client confidentiality.

References

1   https://early.app/blog/remote-working-affects-productivity/
2   www.globallegalpost.com/news/global-law-firms-boosted-uk-productivity-during-pandemic-study-finds-1607118626
3   www.understandingsociety.ac.uk/blog/2025/06/25/covid-work-wellbeing/
4   https://en.wikipedia.org/wiki/Great_Resignation
5   www.fnlondon.com/articles/us-law-firms-push-staff-back-to-the-office-there-is-a-pendulum-swing-9f776bcf
6   https://ics.uci.edu/~gmark/chi08-mark.pdf
7   www.forbes.com/sites/jackkelly/2021/04/05/indeed-study-shows-that-worker-burnout-is-at-frighteningly-high-levels-here-is-what-you-need-to-do-now/
8   www.lawcare.org.uk/media/14vhquzz/lawcare-lifeinthelaw-v6-final.pdf
9   www.legal500.com/future-lawyers/2024/11/14/how-much-do-nq-solicitors-earn/
10 www.saccomann.com/resources/blog/what-nq-solicitors-value-most-in-a-new-role/

Chapter 6:
AI and time management – a game changer for lawyers

By Sarah Murphy, general manager, Clio International

The six-minute myth is cracking

Ask any lawyer what they need more of, and their answer is almost always the same – time. For decades, we've been told that if we just planned better, delegated more, or used pretty color-coded calendars, we would finally catch up with our mounting backlog. Yet despite all these time management hacks, lawyers remain some of the most time-strapped professionals around. The real issue isn't just how we track our time – it's how much of it gets eaten up by admin, red tape, and constantly keeping up with client demands.

The six-minute billing unit used to be the go-to, but now it feels more like a reminder of how much time gets lost. Updating files, hunting down documents, or chasing client signatures is a constant time sink that steals time away from actual legal work. Trying to cram more into the working day never works because it does not address the core issue. We can try to get better at sorting emails or logging hours, but the mountain of non-billable work just keeps growing.

But AI is changing the game. The latest research shows that 96 percent of law firms have adopted AI in some way.[1] AI isn't just another tool to track time – it's making us rethink how we spend it. Early adopters of AI in law cite efficiency gains as the top benefit.[2] Whether it's reviewing documents, automating billing, or handling scheduling and client intake, AI is quietly taking care of repetitive tasks. According to Thomson Reuters, AI could save lawyers up to four hours a week.[3] That means more time for client care, strategy, or simply taking a breather.

With clients expecting more, regulations becoming tighter, and admin piling up, the old systems just can't keep up. New AI-powered tools are designed for real law firms, helping lawyers streamline workflows, reduce context switching, and make it easier to respond to clients faster without burning out. The six-minute myth is losing its grip. The question is: are you ready to see what happens with all the time you get back?

AI in legal practice – what it really means

Legal AI simply means using smart software to help with legal work. It's not about robots replacing lawyers. It's about supercharging your productivity.

Here's what legal AI can do:

- Scan contracts and flag unusual clauses.
- Draft basic letters or emails.
- Search through thousands of documents.
- Remind you about deadlines.
- Alert you to missing information in cases.

Automation, machine learning, and generative AI – what's the difference?

Automation is the simple, rule-based stuff, using "If X, then Y". One example could be an email rule that moves client intake forms to a designated folder, or a billing system that sends invoices on the last day of the month. Automation follows set instructions with no learning or adapting. This makes it ideal for structured, predictable tasks, but sadly lacking when dealing with unexpected situations.

Machine learning is the next step up. Here the software learns from data, identifies patterns, and makes decisions on its own without needing your input. If you tag a few emails as "urgent", it will start to recognize the defining characteristics and flag similar ones in future. Machine learning powers tools that identify which documents are relevant in discovery, flag non-standard contract clauses, or predict outcomes based on past cases. It encompasses different learning protocols – from labeled data, from sorting unlabeled data, and through trial and error.

Generative AI is the latest tech. Its standout feature is that it can create new content that mimics human creativity. While machine learning models predict or classify, generative AI models produce outputs that did not exist in the original data. These tools can draft emails, summarize case law, or even answer open-ended questions about your own matters. Generative AI is what powers tools like Clio Duo, which can generate a first draft of a client update or pull together a summary of your open cases.

Why AI isn't replacing lawyers

AI isn't here to take your job. It's here to take over your admin. AI can process vast amounts of data quickly and generate initial drafts or research summaries. But it lacks the ability to interpret nuance, understand emotional context, or provide the personalized advice that your clients expect. Legal matters often involve intricate human narratives, ethical considerations, and the need for creative problem-solving. No robot lawyer will ever replace your judgment, advocacy, or client care. What AI does is handle repetitive, time-consuming chores so that you can focus on your real work.

AI also helps reduce "context switching" – the tiresome effort of having to continually switch between apps and tasks. This constant switching is draining on both your time and your concentration. Instead of you constantly bouncing between researching case law, managing client communications, and reviewing contracts, your software can pull everything together for you in one place. You no longer have to manually sift through multiple sources, toggle between documents, and jump around different software platforms.

Finally, when your client asks, "What's going on with my case?" AI can pull up a summary of the latest updates in seconds. AI-powered chatbots and virtual assistants can provide clients with instant progress reports on case status, upcoming deadlines, and recent developments. These tools can also answer routine questions and even send proactive alerts about changes in regulations or court schedules that your client might need to know.

How AI reshapes time management

Whether you're a solicitor, fee earner, legal assistant, or practice manager, you know how hard it is to find enough hours in the day. Between looking after demanding clients and wading through endless admin, it can feel that you never even have time to catch your breath. But AI is no longer a distant idea about the future. It's already transforming the way legal teams work, giving them back hours once lost to repetitive tasks and context switching. Here's four ways in which AI is making a real difference in law firms right now.

Reducing repetitive admin

Let's be honest, you didn't go to law school to spend your days formatting documents or filling out the same forms over and over. Yet this is often the reality and it takes up way too much time. This is where AI is changing things fast.

AI-powered document automation tools can now draft standard letters, contracts, and court forms in seconds. Instead of starting from a template, you just pick a template, answer a few questions, and let AI do the heavy lifting. If you're sending a follow-up email to a client, AI can suggest wording based on your previous emails, saving you the headache of keeping your messaging consistent.

Accelerating legal research and drafting
Legal research and drafting are hugely time-consuming. Digging through case law, statutes, and precedents can take hours or even days. But AI is flipping the script. Currently 36 percent of firms use AI document drafting and automation[4] and 62 percent of firms expect to increase AI use in the next 12 months.[5]

Today's AI-powered research tools can:
- Instantly search and summarize huge databases of case law and legislation.
- Suggest relevant precedents and clauses for contracts or pleadings.
- Flag inconsistencies or missing elements in drafts, ensuring nothing is missed.

Right now, about 29 percent of law firms use AI for contract review and 17 percent use AI for legal research.[6] These numbers are rising as tools become more sophisticated and user-friendly. For example, AI can scan a pile of contracts for key risks or compliance issues in minutes, flagging clauses that need attention and even suggesting fixes.

Time recording made easy
Time recording is never a favorite task. Manual time entry is tedious, easy to mess up, and often means lost billable hours. This is where AI-powered time recording steps in.

The latest tools are changing the game by doing the following:
- Automatically tracking billable work such as emails, drafting documents, calls, and meetings. The work is then logged to the right client or matter.
- Suggesting time entries based on what you've been working on, which you can review and approve with a click, rather than you trying to remember everything at the end of the day.
- Boosting accuracy and also capturing more billable time. Firms using automated time capture report recovering 20 percent more billable hours.[7]

Remarkably, most lawyers only bill 2.9 hours in an eight-hour workday[8] because tracking time is such a hassle. AI-driven time recording closes this gap, cutting down on admin fatigue and boosting revenue.

Reducing context switching

As a lawyer, you're constantly pulled in different directions. You're jumping between cases, answering client calls, and replying to emails. All this "context switching" is a huge drain on your productivity. Every time you switch tasks, it takes you a while to get back up to speed.

AI is tackling this head-on by:

- Instantly summarizing files, emails, and notes so you can quickly get the key points without rereading everything.
- Giving you quick overviews of cases and recent updates, so you can dive back into your work without missing a beat.
- Pulling out the most relevant information right when you need it – client details, deadlines, recent communications – by integrating with your practice management system.

Say you return from a client meeting and need to catch up on a different matter. Instead of digging through endless emails and notes, you ask your AI assistant for a quick summary. Within seconds, you're up to speed and ready to go.

Task management transformed

As a legal professional, the daily onslaught of deadlines, documents, and client communications can often feel overwhelming. No doubt you're spending a big chunk of your day just sifting through information. You've heard the buzz about AI, but it's not just empty hype. With the latest advances in technology, AI has become a practical tool that can transform how you manage your workload, stay focused, and give your clients better service. The following outlines how AI is being used in legal task management today.

Helping you stay focused with email summaries, to-do lists, and deadline reminders

AI tools can scan lengthy emails and documents that would normally take hours to read and give you the main points in seconds. No more reading five-paragraph client updates that sap your precious time and mental energy. Instead, you get a concise summary that saves your brain power for the high-value legal work you were hired to do.

AI tools can go through your communications and case files, identify the required actions, and auto-generate to-do lists. Say a client sends you a list of requested amendments to a contract. Your AI assistant can pull out each task and slot it into your case management system. This keeps everything organized and gives you the peace of mind that nothing has been missed.

Stressing over deadlines is the bane of every lawyer's work. AI tools can help by scanning your calendar, case files, and emails to identify what needs to be done and when. You'll get timely reminders for urgent tasks so nothing gets lost. Now you can stay ahead of court dates and filing deadlines and avoid the kind of costly mistakes that could lose you cases and clients.

Real-world scenario – how AI helps a busy lawyer juggling ten cases

Let's look at how this works in real life. Emma is a busy solicitor working at a mid-sized firm, currently handling ten active cases. Each case has its own stream of client emails, court filings, and internal memos. It's hard to keep up and Emma has to spend hours a week organizing her to-do list and updating case timelines. But that was before AI.

This is how AI enhances Emma's workflow:

- *Inbox triage.* Each morning, Emma's AI assistant goes through her inbox, summarizing long client emails and flagging urgent requests. Emma no longer has to spend time reading every message in full. Instead, she scans the summaries and dives deeper only when needed.
- *Task management.* Emma's AI looks for action items from her emails, like "Draft reply to opposing counsel" or "File amended complaint", then adds them to her to-do list, organized by case.
- *Case timeline updates.* As new court dates, client instructions, and document instructions are received, the AI updates each case's timeline. Any changes are flagged and Emma gets an immediate alert if any deadlines are brought forward.
- *Deadline reminders.* Emma's AI sends her daily digests of upcoming deadlines and overdue tasks. Tasks are arranged in order of priority according to their urgency and importance to the client. She will receive a nudge if she's about to fall behind on any item.
- *Meeting prep.* Before each client call or court hearing, Emma's AI sends her a quick summary, covering recent case activity, key documents, and outstanding tasks. Now Emma always comes fully prepared, even when switching between cases.

With the help of AI, Emma is no longer in a losing battle with her admin. She finally has the time to properly focus on her core strengths of legal analysis, negotiation, and client strategy. This revitalizes her work and her clients notice the extra responsiveness and attention to detail.

Client interaction – better, faster, smarter

The legal world is becoming ever more competitive. Clients are looking for not just expertise, but also responsiveness, clarity, and focus. Meeting these heightened expectations can feel like a high-wire act, especially when time and resources are limited. This is where AI comes into play, not as a replacement for the human lawyer, but as a powerful ally in delivering better, faster, and smarter client interactions.

How AI enhances the client experience

AI can give clients a smoother experience in the following ways:

- *Faster response, real-time answers.* Clients don't want to wait for days for a reply to a simple question. Queries can be answered 24/7 using AI-powered chatbots and virtual assistants, letting clients know that their concerns are being taken seriously.
- *Better communication.* Legal jargon should be avoided as it can cause confusion and reduce trust from clients. AI tools like Clearbrief and WordRake can rework legalese into plain English that lay clients can easily understand.
- *Improved follow-ups.* Following up with clients is hard, especially with a workload of multiple cases. AI-powered practice management platforms like Clio can ensure key dates, deadlines, and follow-ups are not missed.

AI summarizes calls and emails for improved productivity and accuracy

No one wants to spend hours typing attendance notes or going through lengthy email chains. AI tools can produce instant summaries of the relevant information.

- *Meeting summaries.* Tools like Otter.ai and Fireflies.ai transcribe calls and use AI to highlight key points, action items, and deadlines. This saves you time and makes sure that important details are not missed.
- *Email summaries.* Staying on top of client communications is easy when AI can scan email threads and pull out the important information. This is already a feature in some email clients and practice management systems.

The client-centric firm powered by AI

Being a client-centric firm means putting your client experience at the heart of everything you do. Clients notice when their needs are anticipated and every detail is taken care of. This results in higher retention rates and more referrals. AI makes this possible in the following ways:

- *Personalized service.* AI determines client preferences from your data and tailors communications and services accordingly.
- *Proactive engagement.* No more waiting for clients to reach out. AI can nudge you to check in at key stages in a matter.
- *Continuous improvement.* AI tools monitor client satisfaction and feedback, giving you the insights you need to improve your service.

AI tools for enhanced legal timekeeping and practice management

Artificial intelligence (AI) tools are increasingly integrated into legal practice management platforms, offering significant advancements in efficiency and accuracy. A notable example of such an integration is Clio Duo, an AI tool often packaged with comprehensive platforms like Clio Manage, a practice management software. By automating repetitive tasks and providing data-driven analysis, these AI solutions empower legal professionals to optimize their workflows and enhance client service.

The primary benefits of incorporating AI into legal operations include:

- *Increased productivity.* By handling routine administrative tasks, AI frees up valuable time, allowing legal teams to concentrate on complex legal work, strategic thinking, and nurturing client relationships.
- *Reduced errors.* Automated summaries, intelligent data analysis, and AI-assisted drafting capabilities significantly minimize the potential for human error in legal documentation and communication.
- *Improved client experience.* AI tools contribute to faster response times, clearer communication, and proactive follow-ups, leading to greater client satisfaction and stronger relationships.

AI tools typically assist legal teams in several key areas:

- *Summarizing case files and communications.* AI-powered features, exemplified by tools like Clio Duo, can rapidly synthesize large volumes of information, providing concise overviews.
- *Case file summaries.* AI can generate quick summaries of case statuses, recent activities, and key documents, enabling lawyers to grasp the essential details of a matter at a glance.

- *Communication summaries.* These tools can review recent emails, phone logs, and text messages, extracting critical information to provide summaries and identify actionable items, ensuring no important detail is overlooked.
- *Drafting routine communication.* AI, as seen in platforms such as Clio Duo, facilitates the creation of professional and consistent communications.
- *Automated drafts.* AI can draft professional emails and texts, often aligning with a firm's specific voice and style guidelines. These drafts serve as a starting point for lawyers, who can then review, edit, and send them.
- *Error reduction and consistency.* By pulling relevant details directly from a firm's existing data, AI helps reduce the risk of factual errors and ensures consistency across all client and internal communications.
- *Suggesting billable time entries.* AI plays a crucial role in optimizing timekeeping and ensuring accurate billing.
- *Eliminating missed entries.* AI can analyze recent activities, such as calls, emails, and document interactions, to identify and recommend billable time entries that might otherwise be overlooked or forgotten.
- *Reducing manual entry.* By assisting with the tracking and recording of time, AI significantly cuts down on the tedious and time-consuming administrative burden associated with manual time entry.

Getting started with legal AI – a roadmap for lawyers

As a solicitor, fee earner, or practice manager, you'll have heard the hype about AI changing the game in legal practice. You may be feeling a bit overwhelmed by all the options. Understandably, you might not want to dive in without testing the water first. You don't need to overhaul your entire practice or become a tech guru to start seeing the benefits of AI. In fact, starting small is the best way to approach it. Here are our best tips to get you started.

Choose tools built for law firms

There's a huge selection of AI tools on the market, but not all of them are built for legal professionals. Focus on solutions developed specifically for the legal sector as they will come with features and safeguards designed to fit in with your workflow. For example, Kira Systems (for contract review), Luminance (for document analysis), and Clio Duo (for practice management) are built to handle the legal tasks and compliance needs that you face on a day-to-day basis.

Furthermore, legal-specific AI tools are likely to integrate seamlessly with your existing tech and offer proper data security and audit trails. They're also likely to have been refined through use by other law firms, giving you the confidence and peace of mind you need.

Look for integration with existing workflows

You may have concerns that new tools will disrupt the way you already work, but the best AI solutions fit into your current processes. Think of them as assistants for the way you do things, not replacements. For example, AI can plug into your existing document management system to help you summarize files and flag key issues.

When evaluating AI vendors, ask these questions:

- Does your tool work with my current case management or email system?
- Can it automate tasks I'm doing manually, such as drafting standard emails or summarizing documents?
- Is your interface intuitive, or is there a learning curve?

There's no need to learn an entirely new platform. The easier it is to slot AI into your daily routine, the more likely you are to use it.

Start with low-risk, high-reward use cases

You don't have to go all in to reap the benefits of AI. The savviest firms start with simple, low-risk implementations that deliver instant time savings. Here's some ideas on where to get started:

- *Drafting routine emails.* AI-powered drafting assistants can draw up first drafts of client updates, reminders, or follow-ups. All you need to do is review and edit, then send.
- *Summarizing documents and case files.* AI can quickly scan and summarize long and complex documents, enabling you to get up to speed faster before important meetings.
- *Extracting key dates or clauses.* Some tools will pull out renewal dates, important clauses, and deadlines from contracts. No more worries about missing something critical.

These examples are low-stakes, yet they add up to measurable time savings every week.

Time to take back your time

The legal profession is one in which every minute counts. AI frees you from the tedious, low-value tasks that you dread to give you time to focus on what really matters – your work, your clients, and your wellbeing. What would you do with just one extra hour each day? This could mean more time for client strategy, business development, or even a quick catch-up with a colleague over coffee. You can start by getting AI to do simple tasks like drafting routine emails, summarizing routine emails, or suggesting billable time entries. Just remember – AI tools are here to support you, not overwhelm you.

References

1   Clio (2024). *The 2024 Legal Trends Report The Latest Legal Trends Report: AI Adoption in UK Law Firms.* www.clio.com/uk/resources/legal-trends/2024-report/ai-adoption-uk-infographic/

2   Calaguas, M. (25 April 2025). *2024 Artificial Intelligence Report.* ABA. www.americanbar.org/groups/law_practice/resources/tech-report/2024/2024-artificial-intelligence-techreport/

3   Thomson Reuters. (16 January 2025). *How AI is Transforming the Legal Profession.* Thomson Reuters. https://legal.thomsonreuters.com/blog/how-ai-is-transforming-the-legal-profession/

4   Clio (2024). *The 2024 Legal Trends Report The Latest Legal Trends Report: AI Adoption in UK Law Firms.* www.clio.com/uk/resources/legal-trends/2024-report/ai-adoption-uk-infographic/

5   *Ibid.*

6   *Ibid.*

7   Sparla, P. (11 November 2024). *Maximizing Efficiency: The Benefits of Automated Time Tracking For Law Firms.* IRIS. www.irisecm.com/blog/maximizing-efficiency-the-benefits-of-automated-time-tracking-for-law-firms/

8   Clio (2024). *The 2024 Legal Trends Report.* www.clio.com/uk/resources/legal-trends/2024-report/

Chapter 7:
The culture of busyness – breaking free from constant overload

By Gary Miles, The Free Lawyer

The hidden epidemic in legal practice

I remember sitting in my car after a particularly grueling day, too exhausted even to start the engine. Despite being at the peak of my career – managing partner of a successful firm, with decades of trial victories behind me – I felt trapped. The very success I had worked so hard to achieve had become a prison of endless demands, constant availability, and chronic overwhelm.

This moment of recognition forced me to confront an uncomfortable truth – I wasn't alone in this struggle. Conversations with colleagues revealed a disturbing pattern across our profession. Accomplished attorneys, from solo practitioners to senior partners at prestigious firms, were quietly drowning in the very practices they had built. They spoke of 80-hour weeks as normal, of checking emails at midnight, of family dinners interrupted by "urgent" client calls that could have waited until morning. This shared experience of overwhelm is a testament to the challenges we all face in the legal profession, and it's crucial that we acknowledge and support each other in this journey.

Somewhere along our professional journey, busyness transformed from an unfortunate side effect of legal practice into a twisted badge of honor. We wear our overwhelm like a symbol of importance, believing that frantic juggling of multiple priorities proves our value and success. This dangerous equation – busyness equals worth – has created a culture where exhausted attorneys mistake activity for achievement.

This chapter examines the hidden forces driving attorney overwhelm and reveals the devastating costs of chronic busyness that many practitioners are unaware of. More importantly, it provides eight battle-tested tools for breaking free from this trap. These tools, developed through decades of legal practice and refined while coaching attorneys who were drowning in professional demands, are invaluable resources in your journey to wellbeing.

The perfect storm creating modern attorney overwhelm

Today's legal profession faces unprecedented pressures that create a perfect storm of overwhelm, with external forces combining to make balance feel impossible for even the most capable attorneys. It's crucial that we recognize the need for balance in our lives, as it is not only a key to our wellbeing but also to our long-term success in this demanding profession.

Technology as taskmaster

The smartphone that promised professional freedom has become our electronic shackle. Unlike previous generations of lawyers who could leave the office and truly disconnect, today's attorneys face relentless pressure to respond immediately across multiple communication channels. The expectation of instant availability has fundamentally changed client relationships. Clients once understood that legal matters required time and patience, but now they expect text-message-speed responses to complex legal questions.

This creates a constant state of alert that prevents lawyers from ever truly stepping away from work. Many attorneys check work email compulsively outside business hours, reporting anxiety when unable to respond immediately to client communications. The boundary between professional and personal time has essentially dissolved.

Economic pressures fueling overcommitment

Billable hour requirements at large firms continue to escalate, with many associates facing demanding annual targets while also engaging in business development activities. Solo practitioners and small firm owners face different but equally intense pressures managing cash flow, accounts receivable, and the constant need to generate new business.

These economic realities create a scarcity mindset where every potential opportunity feels too valuable to pass up. The financial pressure becomes particularly acute during economic uncertainty when clients delay payments or reduce legal spending. Many lawyers respond by taking on more work to compensate for reduced rates, creating an exhausting cycle where increased effort yields diminishing returns.

The client shopping revolution

Modern clients approach legal services like consumers comparing products online. They research attorneys, read reviews, and switch representation more easily than ever before. This shift has created intense competition, driving many lawyers to overcommit rather than risk losing potential business.

Online rating systems and social media have intensified the pressure to please every client perfectly, prompting lawyers to go to extraordinary lengths to accommodate unreasonable requests or impossible timelines. The fear of negative reviews creates a dynamic where attorneys feel compelled to say yes to everything.

The psychological drivers of attorney overwhelm

Beyond external pressures, internal psychological patterns often drive lawyers toward chronic overwhelm, creating self-imposed stress that compounds professional demands.

Perfectionism as professional hazard

Legal education trains attorneys that details matter – lives, fortunes, and freedoms depend on getting things right. While attention to detail is essential for competent representation, many lawyers develop paralyzing perfectionism that makes every task take far longer than necessary.

The fear of making mistakes drives excessive research, endless document revisions, and chronic second-guessing, which unnecessarily multiplies workload. This perfectionist tendency, often reinforced by early academic success, drives attorneys to work far harder than necessary on many projects, spending hours agonizing over single sentences in briefs, convinced that perfect wording will make the difference between winning and losing.

Imposter syndrome in professional practice

Despite impressive credentials and proven track records, many lawyers secretly wonder if they truly deserve their success. Using busyness as proof of value becomes a way to quiet these internal doubts – if constantly busy, one must be important and competent. This creates an addiction to overwhelm where slowing down feels threatening rather than restorative.

Attorneys who have won significant verdicts still question whether they "got lucky" rather than recognizing their skill and preparation. This impostor syndrome drives them to work excessive hours, believing that effort can compensate for perceived inadequacy.

Achievement addiction and external validation

The legal profession attracts high achievers who often derive their primary

sense of identity from professional accomplishments. When external validation becomes the primary source of self-worth, attorneys need constant
activity and recognition to feel valuable. This achievement addiction makes
rest feel like regression and creates chronic dissatisfaction even with significant success.

The devastating hidden costs of chronic busyness

The actual price of constant overwhelm extends far beyond immediate
stress, creating compound damage that affects every aspect of an attorney's
life and effectiveness.

Physical health deterioration

Chronic overwhelm takes a severe toll on an attorney's physical health, with
stress-related symptoms becoming normalized in legal culture. Sleep disrup-
tion affects substantial numbers of lawyers, leading to compromised
immune function, digestive issues, and cardiovascular strain. Many attorneys
survive on caffeine and fast food, skipping regular meals, exercise, and
medical checkups.

Physical symptoms often develop gradually, making them easy to ignore
or rationalize as temporary inconveniences. Tension headaches become
chronic, digestive issues are blamed on "eating on the run", and persistent
fatigue is attributed to "just being busy". By the time attorneys recognize
these as serious health issues, significant damage may already be done.

Mental health crisis in the legal profession

Mental health challenges are widely recognized as disproportionately
affecting the legal profession, with attorneys experiencing higher rates of
addiction, clinical depression, and anxiety disorders compared to other occu-
pations. Despite professional success, many lawyers report feeling
emotionally numb, losing passion for work they once loved, and struggling
with concentration and decision-making abilities.

What's particularly troubling is how the profession normalizes mental
health struggles as "just part of being a lawyer". This cultural acceptance
prevents many attorneys from seeking help until problems become severe,
missing opportunities for early intervention.

The productivity paradox

Research consistently demonstrates that working excessive hours doesn't increase overall productivity – it often decreases effectiveness. The constant task-switching that characterizes overwhelmed attorneys' days requires significant time to refocus after interruptions, meaning constantly busy lawyers spend substantial time in a scattered, inefficient state.

The constant fatigue and scattered attention that result from overwork reduce the quality of output, creating a counterproductive cycle where more effort yields poorer results.

Client service quality decline

Ironically, the busyness intended to demonstrate dedication to clients often undermines the quality of representation provided. Overwhelmed attorneys give scattered attention during client meetings, delay responses despite good intentions, and provide superficial rather than deep engagement with complex legal issues. Clients can sense when they're being treated as just another item on an overwhelming to-do list rather than receiving focused, strategic counsel.

Professional effectiveness erosion

Constant busyness prevents lawyers from stepping back to see the bigger picture, emerging opportunities, or long-term consequences of current decisions. This tactical-only thinking means always reacting to immediate problems rather than building systems that prevent issues from arising. Strategic thinking – essential for business development, case strategy, and career advancement – becomes impossible when every moment is consumed with urgent tasks.

Eight strategic tools for breaking free from overload

Understanding the problem of attorney overwhelm is necessary but insufficient for creating lasting change. Transformation requires specific, actionable strategies for managing time, energy, and professional commitments more effectively.

Tool 1: Conduct your personal time audit

The first step toward intentional practice is understanding where time goes versus where you think it goes. Commit to tracking activities in 15-minute blocks for one complete week, recording everything – client work, email, phone calls, administrative tasks, even transition time between activities.

Crucially, also note the energy level and focus quality for each block. This reveals not just where time goes, but when you're productive versus when you're merely going through the motions. Many attorneys discover they're spending substantial portions of their time on activities that could be eliminated, delegated, or significantly streamlined.

Email processing is often the biggest revelation – lawyers frequently underestimate the cumulative time spent on electronic communication when including all quick checks and responses throughout the day. This data becomes the foundation for making informed decisions about time allocation.

Tool 2: Master strategic time blocking

Time blocking goes beyond basic calendar management to create a systematic approach for protecting important work from constant interruptions that derail productivity. Your brain performs best when it can focus intensely for extended periods. Yet, most lawyers spend days in continuous partial attention, jumping from task to task without achieving the concentration necessary for complex legal thinking.

Block two- to three-hour periods for demanding work requiring real intellectual engagement. During these blocks, make sure you are unavailable for anything short of actual emergencies. Work that previously took all day gets completed in these focused sessions with significantly better quality.

Schedule buffer time – 30-60 minutes daily reserved for unexpected issues that inevitably arise. This buffer time is crucial for maintaining focus on priorities without being derailed by emergencies. Without this planned flexibility, one urgent client call can destroy an entire carefully planned day.

Tool 3: Achieve crystal clear goal setting

Vague aspirations like wanting to "be successful" and "serve clients well" aren't sufficient to guide daily decisions about time and energy allocation. Absolute clarity requires specific, measurable objectives at multiple time horizons.

Work with annual goals covering both professional and personal priorities – specific income targets, types of cases to handle, skills to develop, and life balance objectives. Translate these into quarterly objectives that break annual goals into manageable 90-day chunks, creating urgency that maintains forward momentum. Finally, convert quarterly objectives into weekly priorities – typically three to five key focus areas that guide daily scheduling.

This goal framework becomes powerful when opportunities arise. Instead of making decisions based on fear ("What if I miss out?") or ego ("This sounds impressive"), ask, "Does this align with my weekly priorities and support my quarterly objectives?". This simple question saves countless hours and prevents commitments that pull away from what matters most.

Tool 4: Communicate priorities transparently

One of the most significant sources of lawyer overwhelm comes from others not understanding boundaries and priorities. Weekly team alignment meetings where you share priorities, explain when you need focused time, and clarify what types of decisions they can make independently versus when they should consult you dramatically reduce interruptions while empowering teams to handle more issues autonomously.

Communicate working style to clients from the beginning of the relationship. Explain typical response times for different types of communication, preferred contact methods, and how you structure your schedule to serve them effectively. Most clients appreciate this transparency because it helps them set realistic expectations and understand that organized approaches benefit their cases.

Tool 5: Learn the strategic art of saying no

Fear-based thinking about missing opportunities leads to taking on work that doesn't align with goals or capabilities, ultimately serving no one well. Develop written criteria for evaluating potential new matters. Does this align with practice areas? Is the client willing to respect boundaries? Are timeline expectations realistic? Is the fee structure appropriate for the complexity involved?

Having criteria written down makes consistent decisions easier and helps explain reasoning to potential clients. Address scope creep – when clients request work beyond original agreements – immediately. Absorbing additional work to maintain good client relationships hurts both practice quality and client service effectiveness.

Develop respectful but firm language for declining opportunities that don't meet your criteria. Thank potential clients for considering you, briefly explain why the matter isn't a good fit, and offer referrals to qualified colleagues when appropriate.

Tool 6: Create boundaries that work

Boundaries aren't walls that isolate you from clients and colleagues – they're filters that help focus energy where you can be most effective. Your office set-up can either support focused work or constantly distract you. Minimize visual clutter, organize materials for easy access, and create clear signals when you're unavailable for interruptions.

Manage technology boundaries by turning off non-essential notifications during focused work periods. Set clear start and stop times for work and honor them consistently. Communicate these boundaries to clients and colleagues, and more importantly, respect them yourself.

Learn to separate urgent feelings from truly urgent situations. Just because a client is anxious doesn't mean you need to absorb their stress as your crisis. You can respond professionally and helpfully without taking on their emotional burden.

Tool 7: Make self-care strategic, not selfish

Taking care of yourself isn't selfish – it's strategic. When physically and mentally healthy, you're a better lawyer, leader, and person for everyone in your life. Schedule exercise like any other necessary appointment because physical fitness directly impacts mental clarity and stress resilience.

Sleep is non-negotiable. Poor sleep reduces productivity more than extra working hours provide. Getting seven to eight hours of quality sleep makes you significantly more effective during waking hours. Plan and prepare healthy meals instead of relying on fast food or skipping meals when busy.

Develop stress-reduction techniques that work for your lifestyle – brief walks between meetings, deep breathing exercises during challenging days, and maintaining hobbies and relationships outside the legal profession that provide perspective. When needing additional support, don't hesitate to work with therapists or coaches who understand the unique stresses of legal practice.

Tool 8: Cultivate mindful awareness

Mindfulness isn't about meditation retreats – it's about making conscious choices rather than operating on autopilot. Several times each day, pause and ask, "Am I being intentional about how I'm spending my time right now?" This simple question helps recognize when you've been pulled off course by distractions or when reacting to others' urgencies rather than focusing on priorities.

Learn to recognize physical and emotional responses to stress before they become overwhelming. Early warning signs might include shoulder tension, breathing changes, or feeling mentally scattered. Recognizing these signals allows corrective action before stress impacts performance.

Regularly assess whether daily activities align with stated values and long-term goals. This evaluation helps identify when you've drifted from intended priorities due to external pressures or reactive decision-making.

Creating space for strategic thinking

Strategic thinking – the ability to step back and see the bigger picture – is essential for long-term success, but often becomes the first casualty of busy schedules. Block two to four hours monthly for comprehensive strategic thinking and treat this time as absolutely sacred. During these sessions, review progress toward goals, identify emerging opportunities and challenges, and adjust approaches based on lessons learned.

Hold these sessions away from your regular office to minimize interruptions and create mental space for big-picture thinking. Every week, spend 30 minutes reviewing what worked well, what didn't, and what you learned. This continuous improvement approach helps make minor adjustments rather than waiting for major problems to force significant changes.

Measuring success differently

To truly break free from the culture of busyness, redefine how you measure professional success and personal satisfaction. Instead of tracking billable hours as the primary metric, focus on client satisfaction, successful case outcomes, and referrals from satisfied clients. These quality-focused measures help recognize that excellence often comes from doing fewer things better, rather than doing more things adequately.

Track energy levels at the end of workdays as an indicator of whether your practice is sustainable. If consistently exhausted, something needs to change, regardless of how "productive" you appear to be. Measure presence and engagement in personal relationships rather than just physical attendance at family events.

Implementation strategy

Implementing these eight tools successfully requires a systematic approach. Start with one tool that addresses your most pressing challenge and implement it consistently for 21 days before adding others. This approach builds sustainable habits rather than overwhelming you with too many changes at once.

Most attorneys find success starting with either time auditing (if uncertain where time goes) or time blocking (if needing better focus). Choose based on your biggest current frustration. Share implementation goals with someone who can provide support and accountability – a trusted colleague, coach, or mentor.

Remember that these changes build new neural pathways and professional habits. Some days will feel easier than others, and that's normal. The key is consistency, not perfection.

The choice that defines your career

The many lawyers trapped in chronic overwhelm aren't failures – they're accomplished professionals caught in a cultural trap that equates exhaustion with excellence. This trap is so pervasive that escaping requires conscious effort and strategic planning, but the rewards extend far beyond individual benefit.

When lawyers break free from busyness addiction, they don't just improve their own lives – they model a different way of practicing law for colleagues and the next generation of attorneys. They provide better service to clients through focused attention and strategic thinking. They show their families that success doesn't require sacrificing health and relationships.

The hidden costs of chronic busyness – compromised health, damaged relationships, reduced effectiveness, and lost life satisfaction – represent symptoms of a profession that has lost its way. But this cultural shift began with individual choices, and it can be reversed the same way.

Your decision about how to respond to the overwhelm epidemic will ripple through every aspect of your life and practice. You can continue participating in the collective delusion that busyness equals success, or you can choose the more difficult but infinitely more rewarding path of intentional practice.

The lawyers who choose intentionality don't work less – they work more strategically. They don't serve fewer clients – they serve them more effectively. They don't lower their standards – they focus their excellence where it matters most.

The transformation begins with simple recognition – you have more control over your professional life than the culture of busyness would have you believe. You can choose which clients to serve, which opportunities to pursue, and how to structure your practice. These choices require trade-offs and difficult conversations, but they also create space for the strategic thinking, deep relationships, and meaningful work that make the legal profession truly rewarding.

The busyness trap is real, pervasive, and destructive. But it's not permanent. Based on decades of experience and coaching countless attorneys through this transformation, I am confident that change is possible. The tools are here. The path is clear. Your freedom awaits on the other side of the courage to choose differently.

Chapter 8:
The "always-on" mindset – setting boundaries and managing client expectations

By Mila Trezza, executive coach and former general counsel

Introduction

"Ironically, jobs are actually easier to enjoy than free time, because like flow activities they have built-in goals, feedback, rules, and challenges, all of which encourage one to become involved in one's work, to concentrate and lose oneself in it."
Mihály Csíkszentmihályi[1]

I am having lunch outside when I notice a lovely family of four at the next table. The children are running around, playing, while both parents are glued to their phones. I am guessing, but from the concentration on their faces, they are working. The only time they lift their heads is to ask for the bill.

Later, I return home and send a work email. I receive an out-of-office autoreply saying my recipient is on annual leave. No problem – I make a mental note of when they will be back. But just a few minutes later, I get a detailed reply.

As I wrap up my working day, a colleague mentions they will be on holiday for a few days, but reassures me (twice) that they will be checking their emails regularly.

These moments, so familiar, reveal something that has become common about how we work and live. Why do so many of us feel this almost invincible pressure to be always-on?

Why disconnecting is so difficult

There are many reasons why we find it so hard to disconnect. Some are universal to modern work culture, while others are specific to the legal profession. Some stem from personality traits, such as a tendency towards perfectionism, while others come from work experience and organizational cultures. Often, it is a combination of pressures from various fronts. Below, I have listed some of the reasons I have encountered repeatedly, each of which contributes to our ability, or struggle, to disconnect from work.

Culture

Many legal professionals work in environments where being constantly connected and available is widely accepted. When organizational culture glorifies being "always-on" and tolerates high levels of overload, those behaviors become embedded. These cultures often promote an *"ideal professional prototype"* – someone who is highly responsible and always reachable. Comments like *"Just email Lisa, she always replies straight away"*, or the constant, casual *"Are you busy?"* reinforce the idea that overload equals value, and that constant availability is the path to success. Disconnecting can feel risky.

Business models

In private practice, the billable hours model incentivizes constant productivity. In-house, lean legal teams face pressure to meet internal client demands, often with limited opportunities to delegate. In both scenarios, lawyers are often mindful that slower communication might be perceived as poor service, and performance goals are typically designed to drive – and financially reward – high productivity.

Leadership role models

The boundaries between working hours and personal life are often blurred for many in managerial roles. If junior lawyers rarely see senior professionals setting clear limits or disconnecting, it normalizes overwork and constant availability. If their leaders never switch off – no matter how often they encourage their teams to do so – their behavior sets an example that filters down to the entire team, who then feel they should also respond to emails on weekends and during holidays.

Technology

Technology has enabled us to work from anywhere. It has given us a great degree of flexibility in how we manage of working lives. However, it has also blurred the line between "work" and "home", well before the COVID-19 pandemic.[2] With emails pinging at all hours and notifications grabbing our attention during family meals, it's easy to feel like you ought to respond.

Dedication to work

Many lawyers love what they do. Their dedication often comes from doing work they find fascinating, challenging, and intellectually stimulating, which can make it difficult to switch off.

Workaholism

Workaholism is not simply about working long hours. It is the persistent struggle to psychologically detach from work,[3] often to the detriment of one's health, relationships, colleagues, and ultimately the organization itself. If, for any (valid) reason, work fulfils this role, then the pages that follow may only partly help address the deeper function that "work" is serving.

Legal profession-specific skills

We spend a lot of time zooming in and maintaining tight control over details. Every drafting requires a level of hypervigilance over a significant number of details, double and triple checking, cross-checking, anticipating issues, and thinking deeper. After hours in that analytical mindset, shifting to a more relaxed frame of mind isn't easy.

Significant responsibilities

Significant responsibilities keep us thinking about work constantly, meaning the mental load follows us wherever we go – whether it's the train ride home, dinner with our neighbors, or a family event. We might replay difficult conversations, mentally edit our work, monologue our frustrations, and continue to wrestle with how to solve complex problems.

A perfectionist mindset

Perfectionism is a trait common to many lawyers, and one that is often rewarded and even considered critical for success. This reinforces the drive to be even more perfect over time. But a perfectionist mindset makes switching off much more difficult, because nothing ever feels "good enough" or ready to go. It *has to be* perfect.

However, studies, including those focused specifically on lawyers, consistently show that perfectionism and high self-criticism do more harm than good. Rather than improving professional performance, they are linked to anxiety, depression, and burnout.[4]

Fear of missing out (FOMO)

It's hard to disconnect if you are worried that something important might happen in your absence. Sometimes, FOMO is fueled by organizational culture; other times, it lives mostly in our heads.

Transition challenges

The transition from a junior to a senior role, or from senior to managerial, is often only minimally supported. This transition requires a significant shift, including learning how to prioritize and self-manage a much heavier work-load. Many lawyers continue working in the same way, and with the same level of responsiveness, that served them well earlier in their careers, until they realize they are constantly overwhelmed.

Strategies to reduce being "always-on"

The picture I painted points to a problem that, because it is incremental rather than immediate, many of us tend to deprioritize. But over time, our difficulty in switching off can become such an ingrained habit that it spirals into a 24/7 "always-on" mindset, one that affects our wellbeing and ultimately undermines the very productivity we are aiming to achieve.

We want to be ultra-productive by making use of every available minute. But fatigue (including internet fatigue),[5] stress, and the frustration that comes from overcommitment leave us tired, overwhelmed, unable to relax and, ultimately, less productive.

We become exactly what we have tried so hard to avoid.

Start with boundaries

Are boundaries a good place to start? Yes, primarily because boundaries are within our sphere of control. While changing the culture in our workplace, or even the wider legal profession, is important, it requires a much broader, collective, and gradual effort. By contrast, setting new boundaries or healthier boundaries than the ones we already have is not quick and easy, but it is progress that is within everyone's reach.

For the purpose of this chapter, my own definition of boundaries is this – *important rules you establish for yourself to enable you to perform at your best, enjoy what you do, and continue to grow.*

Without boundaries, life becomes chaotic and overwhelming. Have you ever tried to discuss something with someone who keeps taking every incoming call?

Things may get done, but you often feel a lot is out of your control – and in reality, it is. You may find yourself trying to be in two places at once (work and home included), constantly swept along by whoever comes first. Without boundaries, it is hard to grow because you are always struggling to carve out time for yourself.

My formula for setting or resetting boundaries might be simple, but hopefully, it provides a starting point even in the most challenging situations. It is never too late, and some progress is always within reach.

But before considering what boundaries might look like, pause for a moment and ask yourself honestly, are you truly committed to prioritizing what those boundaries are meant to protect? Are you ready to keep your eyes on the prize – more time, your wellbeing, and the many other dimensions of life beyond work?

Step one: Define your boundaries

Your first step in setting boundaries is to take a long look in the mirror and identify those habits you have built over time that no longer allow you to truly devote yourself to your priorities. Chances are, they benefit neither your wellbeing nor your work.

Boundaries are personal, but here is a starting list of rules you might consider adopting. Now, exceptions are also subjective, so how you judge what you allow as an exception to your rules is fundamental. As a general rule to your rules, "urgent" should not be a daily occurrence.

Here are some example boundaries you might consider experimenting with:

- No work during weekends. If full weekends off are not realistic, especially during intense periods, choose at least one day or half-day (say, Saturday or Sunday) when you intentionally decide not to work.
- No work after 6pm, 7pm, or whatever time makes sense for your role. The key is to define a realistic point when you disconnect.
- Have a "no meeting" day per week, if your schedule allows. Use that day to focus on your most challenging tasks.
- No emails while on holiday. If that's not feasible, consider limiting yourself to, say, one hour of email checking in the evening.
- No interruptions during high-focus tasks like writing or meetings. Your phone is on silent.
- Lunch breaks of at least 30-45 minutes, or whatever duration is achievable for you.
- No work phone calls or emails during your meals.
- No emails before breakfast, morning exercise, or whatever your morning routine is.
- Mid-morning and mid-afternoon breaks, even if only a few minutes, to reset.

- Clear your desk, write your priorities for tomorrow, and shut down your devices at the end of your working day. Rituals are a way to make boundaries visible to you.
- Mute notifications from as many apps as possible that do not need your immediate attention.
- Use a separate phone for personal and work communication if it helps to leave work at home during your non-working hours.
- No work phone calls during social events. Your presence matters.

Step two: Communicate your boundaries

Many years ago, I worked with a lawyer in private practice who, first thing in the morning, would record a voicemail setting out his availability for the day. It went something like this:

"This is the voicemail of [name and surname]. I'm in the office today but in meetings all morning and back at my desk after 2pm. Please leave a message, and I'll return your phone call later today. Alternatively, if you need to speak to someone urgently, please contact [name of PA or another person in the firm]."

I was their client at the time, and I thought he did a great job managing my expectations. What also worked well, and we'll talk about this more in step three, is that my phone call was returned exactly when the voicemail said it would be. The communication system was reliable. The point is, not all boundaries need to be communicated. But those that do (usually around our availability) benefit greatly from being clearly stated.

Clear communication serves two key purposes:

- It gives direction to the people who are looking for us – so they know when we're available.
- It gives us peace of mind, knowing that those who need to know now do know.

Below follow some simple ways to communicate availability-related boundaries.

In person, verbally

This works well for things like holidays or time away from work, especially when we want to tell specific people directly. For example, *"If something urgent comes up while I'm away, please call me or leave a voicemail – don't email – as I won't be checking emails."*

Out-of-office autoreply

Out-of-office messages are helpful not only when you are on leave, but also when you are in an all-day meeting. That said, if you don't intend to reply, or if someone is covering you, your out-of-office message needs to be clear. Sometimes, they are not, and may even sound like an invitation to send the email anyway. For example, if your message says you will have *"intermittent access to email"*, your client is still likely to expect a reply. If "away" means you will reply on your return, then the most effective out-of-office message – the one that leaves no doubt – states that you are currently out of the office and will not have access to your email until [exact date].

Voicemail for those who tend to communicate by phone

If you like the idea and don't mind updating your voicemail regularly, it can be a helpful (and personable) way to set expectations.

A note in your email signature

It's now common for people who work part-time to indicate their working days in their signature block, for example, *"My working days are Tuesday, Wednesday, and Thursday".*

Clients might need plenty of reminders about this and may still get confused for a while. But over time (if you stick to your boundaries), they will learn that you don't work on Fridays. What matters is that your communication is consistent and clear.

I once received an email from a lawyer whose signature block said something like, *"Sometimes I send emails outside normal working hours; this doesn't mean I expect a response outside your normal working hours".*

I'm not sure this language works well in a client context. It seems more suited to addressing the possibility that I (the client on this occasion) might feel pressured to respond, rather than providing clarity about when *they* will reply. This wording might work better in a manager-to-team setting, where it can serve as a reminder that, while the manager may work flexibly outside normal hours, there is no expectation for the team to do the same.

Step three: Walk the talk

For many people, this is the hardest part – it involves not just *saying* it, but *doing* it. This includes not answering your emails if you indicated that you were not to be contacted during your days off. Let's walk through a couple of examples when holding the line may require a bit more effort.

Holding boundaries with a boundary-pushing colleague
A colleague asks for *"just ten minutes"* of your time, which turns into a full hour. Or they pop into your office unannounced and unload the last three years of their relationships. That is not how you planned to spend your time today. So, what can you do when someone doesn't respect your boundaries? Here are a few suggestions:

- State your limit upfront – and stick to it. At the start, state your boundary: *"I only have ten minutes right now."* Then, stick to it. Politely, but firmly, wrap up the conversation when those ten minutes are up. Your colleague might try *"just one last thing"*, but the answer remains, *"not now".*

- Redirect the conversation – don't explain. If you are happy to talk, but now really is not a good time, avoid starting the conversation. Suggest another time (or day) to meet: *"I cannot right now, but I have half an hour after 5pm".* Don't get entangled in explaining why you don't have time or listing all the things you need to do. That explanation is not needed.

Managing expectations with the over-demanding client
You may need to try a few approaches with an over-demanding client before finding a workable balance.

One way to move things forward, and gradually build (some) trust, is to spell out, step by step, what you will do and what will happen next, while regularly checking in to confirm that this meets their expectations. At this stage, you are mirroring their need for control, as over-demanding clients rarely settle for a simple *"Just leave it with me".*

Meeting them where they are may be a more effective way to progressively build the working relationship. For example, *"I understand you would like an answer as soon as possible, ideally by Friday. I will call Person A and arrange a meeting to discuss [your matter] with them, and I will provide you with an update by Friday. Would that work for you?"* Of course, the over-demanding client is unlikely to change their approach overnight. Your goal here is nonetheless to reduce your own stress level by avoiding being drawn into their "everything-now" working style. If you are asked the same thing twice, push back: *"We have already discussed that and agreed to do X by tomorrow. Does this still work for you?"* Over time, these interactions can improve.

One final thought. When handling difficult conversations, speak in person or on the phone. You will save yourself a lot of stress and time – anxiety and confusion are rarely resolved through email.[6]

More strategies to break the "always-on" cycle

More strategic no's
Most junior solicitors are told they need to learn to say "no". But the moment that sentence ends, they are inundated with requests and left wondering how to put that advice into practice. Saying "no" goes beyond saying "not now". It means deciding that something (a new matter, a social activity, a volunteering opportunity, or anything else that demands your time and attention) is *not* a priority. It means you have taken the time to identify your top one or two priorities, whether for the week or the month or the year, and to prune out the unnecessary so you can focus on what truly matters to you.

Don't just communicate – listen
As Adair put it, "Listening has been called the forgotten skill in communication".[7]

While it is important to communicate to your client what exactly you are going to do and by when, it is equally important that they feel listened to and understood.

Good listening paves the way for many things, including a reasonable deadline. The more distracted we are, the more we interrupt, and the less present we are with a client or team member, the more likely they are to escalate the urgency of their issues to get our attention.

Conclusion
"If you are pained by any external thing, it is not this thing that disturbs you, but your own judgment about it. And it is in your power to wipe out this judgment now."
Marcus Aurelius, *Meditations*

We began by examining the various factors that keep us always feeling "on", highlighting the immense pressure we face. From there, we asked not whether it *must* be this way, but more importantly, whether *we want* it to be. If the honest answer is *no*, this chapter will have offered some practical strategies – regularly redefining our boundaries, communicating them clearly, and remembering that we are the gatekeepers of those boundaries. We concluded with a reminder about listening.

You might wonder why listening to others when maintaining boundaries often means others do not listen to us? For two reasons.

First, if we listen and understand our clients' and colleagues' challenges, we are better equipped to develop plans that address their real issues, not just their requests. This enables us to focus our energy effectively, avoiding the overwhelm of doing things twice or the frustration of going off track.

Second, practicing listening to others complements listening to ourselves, including all the signals our body sends when we are tired, need a break, or simply need to disconnect for a while.

Lastly, it is never too late to realize that true productivity does not come from filling every minute. As our professional and personal lives evolve, we can build new boundaries or reset those we have outgrown. And this time, the rewards come with no limits, no boundaries at all.

References

1   *Flow, the Psychology of Happiness*, Mihály Csíkszentmihályi, 2022
2   "How Different Personality Types Cope with an Always-On Culture", John Hackston, *Harvard Business Review*, June 2020
3   "How Being a Workaholic Differs from Working Long Hours – and Why That Matters for Your Health", Lieke ten Brummelhuis and Nancy P. Rothbard, *Harvard Business Review*, March 2018
4   www.nalp.org/the_perfectionist_paradox_webinar
5   *(Dis)Connected How to Stay Human in an Online World*, Emma Gannon, 2022
6   *Difficult Conversations: How to Discuss What Matters Most*, Douglas Stone, Bruce Patton and Sheila Heen, 2011
7   *The Best of Adair on Leadership and Management*, John Adair, 2008

Chapter 9:

Neuroproductivity – mastering your mind to master your time

By Anna Marra, consultant and trainer

"Time is a brisk wind, for each hour it brings something new."
Paracelsus

Have you ever been advised to use time management techniques and felt like they just didn't work for you? If so, don't worry. It's not a coincidence. There are two key factors that improve time management – understanding how your brain works and recognizing that managing time is not about applying a single technique, but about building a system, both internal and external.

Master your mind, master your time
In the fast-paced legal world, where every minute counts, the real key to effective time management isn't just found in calendars, planners, or apps. Instead it's found in the brain. This chapter offers a new perspective – managing time through neuroproductivity, which means aligning our decisions, habits, and rhythms with the brain's natural functioning to achieve more with less stress.

Neuroscience is a scientific discipline focused on studying the nervous system, especially the brain. This multidisciplinary field brings together biology, chemistry, psychology, medicine, and computer science, all aimed at understanding how the brain works and how its functions influence behavior and cognitive abilities. Neuroscience provides us with a deep understanding of how the brain operates and how to optimize its performance. By applying neuroscientific principles, we can develop effective strategies to enhance our productivity.

Time management is crucial for both productivity and overall wellbeing. From a neurological standpoint, the brain plays a central role in how we perceive, organize, and use time. Understanding these brain processes can lead to more effective strategies for time management.

Why can neuroscience make us more productive? Unlike traditional methods, neuroscience doesn't offer generic "productivity hacks", but rather strategies grounded in how the brain actually functions.

It helps us understand, for example:

- How attention and motivation work.
- What disrupts our ability to concentrate.
- Why we procrastinate or fall into perfectionism.
- How to manage our mental and energetic rhythms throughout the day.

How we perceive time – what your mind does with minutes

Why is it essential to understand how we perceive time to manage it effectively?

Because we don't manage real time, we manage perceived time.

Even though the clock moves forward objectively, our mind experiences time subjectively, influenced by attention, emotions, motivation, and memory. This distortion is critical – if we don't understand how the brain interprets time, we're likely to make poor decisions about how to use it.

You've probably noticed that:

- When you're focused, time flies.
- When you're bored or stressed, time drags.
- When you're doing new things, the day feels longer (more memories are formed).
- When you're on autopilot, the days seem to "disappear".

What happens if we ignore this? If we're unaware of these mechanisms, we're likely to underestimate how much time we actually need, plan poorly, overload ourselves or procrastinate, and end up feeling like there's "never enough time" – even when, objectively, there could be.

We can only manage time well when we understand how we experience it. It's not about having more hours in a day, but about living them more consciously, with focus and meaning.

The subjective dimension of time perception

Time is not experienced in a linear or objective way – rather, it depends on several factors, such as:

- The level of attention we give it (when you're in a flow state, time "flies").

- The amount of dopamine released (which can lead us to underestimate or overestimate duration).
- The memories we form (the more meaningful events we experience, the "longer" the day feels).
- The emotions we feel (stress and boredom distort time perception).

Neuroscience shows that we can train our perception of time and, by doing so, we improve our ability to prioritize, plan, and make decisions.

But let's take a step back. What's happening in the brain when we perceive time?

Time perception is a subjective phenomenon that varies depending on context and individual differences. The brain uses both internal and external cues to track time, allowing us to organize tasks, plan for the future, and recall past events. Multiple brain systems work together to create a coherent sense of time.

For example, the cerebellum plays a central role in time precision and temporal coordination, while the prefrontal cortex helps maintain and manipulate temporal information in working memory – enabling us to organize actions and anticipate future outcomes. The prefrontal cortex is also crucial for task switching and prioritization, which are essential for effective time management.

The amygdala, part of the limbic system and involved in emotional regulation, can also alter our perception of time, especially in stressful or emotionally charged situations. In moments of fear or anxiety, time may appear to slow down – a phenomenon known as temporal dilation, which highlights the interplay between our emotional and temporal systems. Thus, emotional state and motivation also influence time perception.

The hippocampus also contributes by organizing events into chronological sequences, allowing us to remember when things happened and how they relate to one another. This capacity is fundamental to planning and decision-making because it provides temporal context to memory.

Beyond brain regions, other elements shape how we perceive time.

Think back. Have you ever felt time "fly" while crafting arguments for a high-stakes trial? Or, on the contrary, felt time crawl during an endless meeting where nothing of substance was discussed?

That's attention at work. Our ability to concentrate significantly shapes how we experience time. When fully immersed in a stimulating task, time speeds up – another form of temporal dilation. In contrast, when we're bored or disengaged, time drags due to lower cognitive activation.[1]

According to Michael Shadlen, professor of neuroscience at Columbia University and an expert on the neural mechanisms of decision-making, the brain anticipates future events through mental "horizons" – like the end of a sentence or the resolution of a story. When we're focused, the brain actively seeks these horizons, creating the sensation that time is passing quickly. But when boredom dominates, our horizons narrow to the immediate moment, giving us the sense that time is slowing down.[2]

The brain uses the dorsolateral prefrontal cortex to manage attentional resources, filter out distractions, and organize behavior according to temporal demands. This process is key to maintaining an accurate perception of time and achieving efficient cognitive performance. When we are deeply immersed in a task, this state of flow allows the brain to function more efficiently, enhancing productivity while reducing the perception of elapsed time. However, during low-arousal situations, the lack of stimulation reduces activity in this area, diminishing our ability to stay focused and distorting time perception.

Why does painting or playing basketball on a Sunday morning feel like it ends in a flash? Engaging in enjoyable activities makes the brain perceive time as shorter. This is because dopamine, the neurotransmitter linked to pleasure, also plays a crucial role in regulating attention and time perception. It reinforces motivation and focus when we're involved in rewarding tasks. That's why our sense of time varies depending on the emotional and motivational context.

Memory also plays a central role in time management. The hippocampus organizes memories into a chronological sequence, which is essential for planning and carrying out future tasks. The interaction between the hippocampus and the prefrontal cortex allows the brain to integrate temporal information to coordinate actions effectively. Episodic memory, which lets us recall specific events and their temporal context, is critical for anticipating future actions, while prospective memory helps us remember to perform tasks we've planned.

A study[3] published in *Current Biology* showed that neural activity in the anterior cingulate cortex encodes time not through an internal clock, but via the cumulative recording of experiences. In other words, the brain interprets time based on the number of events it processes, not the objective passage of time. When experiences are repetitive or scarce, neural variability decreases, resulting in a shorter subjective duration. This is why routine diminishes the sense of novelty and makes time seem to pass more quickly.

However, incorporating novelty – through travel, new routines, or learning experiences – supports the formation of denser memories, which slows down subjective time perception.

Excessive smartphone use fragments attention and impairs episodic memory, or the ability to remember events in sequence. Recent studies have shown that digital multitasking reduces deep memory encoding, making time feel faster and less meaningful. Divided attention caused by devices interrupts the continuity of experience – time no longer feels like a flowing line but becomes a sequence of interruptions.[4]

In contrast, practices like mindfulness, which engage brain regions involved in time perception – such as the insula and the prefrontal cortex – reduce mental dispersion and increase bodily awareness. As a result, time is experienced as richer or denser, though not necessarily longer. Just as technology tends to dissolve the sense of the present moment, mindfulness tends to expand it.

Stress also alters time perception. Elevated levels of cortisol, the primary stress hormone, can disrupt the functions of the prefrontal cortex and hippocampus, impairing planning, decision-making, and memory. Stress management techniques like meditation and mindfulness can help regulate the stress response and enhance both time perception and time management.

How to use perception to your advantage

Once we understand that we're not managing chronological time, but rather our experience of time, we can adopt strategies that are more effective, realistic, and aligned with how the brain actually works. Below are several strategies that can help:

- *Batch similar tasks to maintain stable mental horizons.* The brain anticipates "mental endpoints". Constantly switching between activities (e.g., from reviewing a contract to preparing for trial, then jumping into a call) breaks that continuity, making everything feel longer and more exhausting. Try grouping similar tasks into focused blocks (e.g., 90 minutes solely for contract review, followed by a break, then phone calls). This supports mental rhythm and creates a stronger sense of real progress.
- *Include enjoyable or creative tasks to make time "fly".* A call with an inspiring client, some creative writing, or a moment to brainstorm strategy can all activate dopamine –boosting focus and making time

feel shorter. If your entire day feels dry or monotonous, your brain gets bored, and time drags.

- *Design your days to avoid going into autopilot mode.* When the brain slips into routine, it stops "recording" moments, leading to the sensation that days evaporate. Shake things up with changes in environment, meeting formats, or your daily agenda. Try having coffee somewhere new, walking while on calls, or experimenting with a new tool. Novelty slows down perceived time and improves memory of the day.
- *Avoid purposeless meetings – they're black holes of time perception.* Activities without direction and fragmented attention feel endless. Push for shorter meetings with a clear end time and active participation. Better yet, reduce meetings altogether and try alternatives like a video, written note, or voice message.
- *Practice mindfulness before or after demanding tasks.* Mindfulness enhances present-moment awareness and "densifies" lived time. Before starting a negotiation or drafting an important document, take three minutes of conscious breathing. Afterward, close your eyes and mentally review what you've accomplished. This helps your brain consolidate the experience.
- *Use the Pomodoro Technique to regulate your perception of effort.* Working nonstop builds tension, while working in short blocks gives the brain micro-rewards and regulates dopamine. Alternate 25 minutes of focused work with five minutes of rest. Each completed block reinforces a sense of progress, and breaks help restore mental energy without losing focus.
- *Minimize phone use and digital multitasking.* Fragmented attention makes the day feel short, but unsatisfying. Create "no-notification zones" (e.g., from 10am to 12pm). Pick one task, silence your phone, and re-experience what it feels like to be 100 percent present. That's how time becomes deep and meaningful, not shallow and scattered.

If the mind structures time based on what it experiences, then we can intentionally design our days so that time not only "works", but feels more valuable.

How we manage time – rhythms, neurofocusing, and strategies
The challenge of managing time is something we face daily. There are well-

known techniques like the Pomodoro Method or the Eisenhower Matrix, but they don't always apply, at least not in every situation and not for every person. We are far too complex as human beings. Your unique genetic makeup is one in trillions – the scope of the number is almost impossible to fathom. Add to that the effects of random mutations and epigenetic factors, and the number becomes astronomical. It's unrealistic to expect one technique to work the same way for everyone with the same level of success.

Instead, it makes more sense to begin with how our brain functions – how it adapts to different situations, how it concentrates, and how it makes decisions.

In the following sections, we'll explore our biological rhythms and how respecting them helps us assign tasks more effectively; how we are electrical beings, and how our brainwaves can activate states of focus (Beta waves) or distraction (Alpha waves); and how attention, as a limited and valuable resource, is central to time management, especially in the face of multitasking, which lowers performance and increases stress.

This last factor, attention, is fundamental to managing time well. Attention is the filter through which we manage time – we can only manage what we pay attention to. If your attention is scattered, time dissolves – you may do a lot, but achieve very little. If your attention is focused and sustained (concentration), time condenses – you do fewer things, but with greater impact.

Let's begin with biological rhythms.

We are rhythmic beings

Circadian rhythms are biological cycles of approximately 24 hours that regulate many bodily functions, including sleep. During nighttime rest, the brain carries out essential tasks like consolidating memory, clearing toxins, and restoring energy. Memory consolidation involves processing and storing the day's information, which supports learning and retention. This is why poor sleep doesn't just affect mood, but also impairs concentration, decision-making, and productivity. Understanding this invites us to see nighttime not as an artificial extension of the day, but as a real time for recovery. Working late or sleeping too little isn't a sign of dedication – instead, it reduces our performance in the medium- and long-term.

Additionally, the brain operates on ultradian rhythms – shorter cycles lasting between 90 and 120 minutes, which regulate our levels of energy, attention, and focus throughout the day. During peaks of activation, we are more creative and efficient; during low phases, we tend to feel fatigue or mental drift.

Respecting these cycles allows us to organize daily work more effectively – assigning demanding tasks to high-energy periods, and reserving routine or light tasks for natural downturns. Including regular breaks aligned with these rhythms not only enhances performance but also prevents mental exhaustion.

In short, the better we understand our internal rhythms, the better we can manage our time and abilities.

We operate on brainwaves

The brain functions through complex electrical communication between neurons. These electrical impulses manifest as what we know as brainwaves – measurable patterns that reflect different mental states. Today, we know that working directly with brainwaves, rather than only with brain chemistry, is a faster and often more effective way to modulate cognitive performance.

Why is this important? Because brain electricity is malleable. We can influence it to promote states such as focus, calm, or rest. This is directly related to the principle of neuroplasticity – the brain's ability to reorganize its structure and neural connections based on experience and training.

Each type of brainwave is associated with a specific mental state, depending on its frequency (measured in hertz, or Hz). For example, if we want to focus, we need the brain to shift from a distracted state to producing faster waves associated with sustained attention. Understanding and respecting these states allows us to work with the brain, not against it.

Broadly speaking, we distinguish five main types of brainwaves:

- *Hi-Beta (above 30 Hz):* maximum alertness and stress – predominant in situations of urgency or anxiety.
- *Beta (12–30 Hz):* associated with active attention, problem-solving, and mental concentration.
- *Alpha (8–12 Hz):* a calm, relaxed state – ideal for creative activities or moments of peace after intense effort.
- *Theta (3.5–8 Hz):* deep relaxation, daydreaming, and creativity – common during meditation or just before sleep.
- *Delta (1–3 Hz):* the slowest waves, linked to deep, restorative sleep and emotional regulation.

Time management is intimately tied to brainwaves, as they determine our mental state and productivity level at any given moment. As we've seen, Beta waves (alert) support analytical thinking and are ideal for complex tasks; Alpha waves (relaxed alertness) foster creativity and strategic thinking; and Theta waves (slower) support deep, intuitive insights.

But the brain doesn't shift frequencies on its own – it needs internal or external stimuli to do so. Let's look at a few examples.

To activate Beta waves (an analytical focus state useful for writing legal documents, analyzing cases, or preparing for trial), you can start with a clear task list (this reduces uncertainty and prevents slipping into high-beta stress); listen to high-frequency rhythmic music with no lyrics; stimulate yourself physically (a cup of coffee, a five-minute walk, deep breathing); or eliminate digital and visual distractions.

To access Alpha waves (a relaxed, focused state that supports strategic thinking, problem-solving, and planning), you can practice slow breathing or short meditation (three to five minutes – you do have them); look out a window (looking into the distance relaxes the visual cortex); take a short break after an intense task (a micro-disconnection), or listen to soft music or nature sounds. What's great is that these don't even have to be real – research has shown that listening to nature recordings or even looking at images of nature can activate Alpha waves.

To stimulate Theta waves (a state of introspection and deep insight, ideal for unlocking ideas or visualizing solutions), you can take hot showers (though not always practical in an office!); go for quiet walks or allow yourself moments before sleep; try freewriting without judgment (a "brain dump"); listen to low-frequency, repetitive music, or practice nasal breathing slowly and consciously (heart coherence techniques).

Shifting your mental state is entirely possible with training. All you need is to identify which brainwave state best supports your current task and apply the right stimulus to "tune" into it. And in case you're skeptical, all of this is measurable, through tools like EEGs (electroencephalograms) and functional MRI scans.

Attention, concentration, and neurofocusing

To continue building on these ideas, we need to clarify three key concepts – attention, concentration, and neurofocusing. Although we often use these terms interchangeably in everyday conversation, they have distinct meanings.

- *Attention* is the ability to select certain stimuli and filter out others. It's the mental "radar" that decides where to direct the mind.

- *Concentration* is sustained attention on a single task over an extended period. It's the mental "zoom" that holds the focus in place.
- *Neurofocusing* is the strategic and conscious use of attention, based on how the brain works. It involves managing rhythms, distractions, and environments to maximize focus and productivity.

The human brain processes around 11 million bits of information per second from the environment. In this sea of stimuli, focusing attention on one specific thing is almost a mental balancing act. This is where the prefrontal cortex comes in – it acts as an intelligent filter, allowing us to direct attention selectively and continuously; what we call concentration.

Our brain, composed of about 100 billion neurons, communicates via electrical impulses that generate brainwaves. Every thought, emotion, or behavior corresponds to a particular frequency. During deep concentration, Beta waves predominate, which are associated with focused mental activity. However, the brain cannot remain in the Beta state indefinitely – it needs pauses to restore energy and maintain proper regulation. That's why alternating periods of cognitive effort with adequate rest – and sleeping well at night – is not a luxury; it's a biological necessity for regaining focus and working efficiently.

So, how do we manage to focus and maintain sustained attention?

The battle for attention and concentration

Attention is the filter that determines which part of reality reaches our mind. When you choose to focus on something, you are intentionally leaving everything else out. That choice is empowering, but it's not always within your control. Often, attention is directed automatically, pulled by external stimuli or internal thoughts. That's why it's said that the quality of your life depends on where you place your attention – what you feel, think, and do is directly shaped by it.

We live in a constant tug-of-war between what we want to focus on and what the environment demands. Well-managed attention becomes a powerful tool to organize time and boost productivity. Concentration is the highest form of attention – it means focusing intentionally and continuously on a single task while blocking out everything else. But it doesn't happen automatically. The brain needs to believe it's worth the effort. Naturally, our mind tends to wander as its priority is survival, not efficiency.

To concentrate, the brain needs two basic conditions – safety and energy.

If it perceives a threat – whether due to stress, urgency, emotional pressure, or task overload – it will activate its alert system and sabotage your focus. That's why creating a calm, low-stimulus, safe environment is key to reduce the temptation to become distracted.

Like a muscle, concentration can be trained. And the brain remembers – if it has successfully focused under certain conditions before, it will tend to replicate that pattern. That's why pre-performance rituals (like those before shooting a free throw in basketball) help us "enter the bubble" of focus. Creating that mental space – safe, energized, and clearly directed – is essential for the brain to generate Beta waves, which support deep attention. Breathing, environment, and motivation act as powerful triggers. And the more you practice entering that bubble, the easier it becomes to return to it.[5]

Multitasking and the age of distraction

Although we often believe that doing many things at once makes us more productive, science shows the opposite. The human brain is not wired for intensive cognitive multitasking. What actually happens is a constant switching of focus, which comes at a cost, known as the *switching cost* – every time we jump from one task to another, we lose rhythm, efficiency, and mental clarity.

For a lawyer, this translates into avoidable mistakes, mental fatigue, and the feeling of not getting anywhere, even after a day of being busy. Studies have shown that after an interruption, the brain can take up to 20 minutes to regain its prior level of concentration. This lost time doesn't just reduce quantity – it impacts the quality of the work.

Chronic multitasking fragments attention, increases stress, lowers information retention, and interferes with decision-making. Recent research shows that over 60 percent of professionals feel this habit negatively impacts both performance and wellbeing. Frequent task-switching overwhelms the brain, especially during complex tasks that require deep focus. The hidden cost of distraction isn't just in wasted minutes – it shows up in poorer work quality. Constantly alternating focus leads to more errors and oversights – it's easy to miss critical details when your mind is always "context switching".[6]

By contrast, training attention to focus on a single task at a time, what we now call *Neurofocusing*, enables us to reach a state of flow – a state of deep concentration in which the mind aligns fully with what it's doing, time perception fades, and productivity reaches its peak.

Psychologist Daniel Goleman, author of *Focus: The Hidden Driver of Excellence*, warns that attention is an underrated yet essential mental asset, vital for success in both life and business.[7]

Neuroscience is clear – when it comes to tasks requiring deep focus, the brain doesn't work in parallel, it works in serial mode. Even if we believe we're multitasking, the brain is actually switching rapidly between tasks, turning circuits on and off. This constant switching causes micro-interruptions that fragment thought and break the flow of work.

The concept of *flow* was developed by Hungarian-American psychologist Mihály Csíkszentmihályi, one of the founders of positive psychology. He defined *flow* as a state of total immersion in a challenging yet stimulating activity, where time seems to disappear and performance reaches its highest level. His research showed that accessing this state boosts both productivity and personal satisfaction, making it a key resource for high-performance professional work.[8]

Innovative companies are already embracing this philosophy. Initiatives like "no-meeting days" or corporate mindfulness programs have shown significant improvements in efficiency, focus, and employee wellbeing. When the mind is freed from noise, it can truly think, decide, and create with clarity.[9]

Focusing on one task at a time doesn't just improve outcomes, it also reduces stress, restores mental clarity, and enhances satisfaction. When we shut the door to distractions, the brain relaxes, cortisol levels drop, and calm returns. Sometimes, completing just one meaningful task is enough to ease the anxiety triggered by everything else on your list.

Neurofocusing

It's fascinating to explore why neurofocusing works so well. Brain science shows us that attention acts like the conductor of our mental orchestra – when it leads effectively, all the "musicians" (memory, creativity, reasoning) play in harmony. When there's no direction, what emerges is noise.

Researchers at Harvard used brain imaging (fMRI) to observe that after just eight weeks of mindfulness training, there was a reduction in the density of gray matter in the amygdala, the brain region central to stress and anxiety responses. At the same time, there was an increase in the density of areas related to attention and emotional regulation. In short, regularly focusing the mind can literally weaken the brain's stress center.

Further research has even found that people accustomed to intense multitasking show lower gray matter density in areas like the anterior cingulate cortex, which is involved in emotional control and decision-making. This suggests that chronic distraction doesn't just cause momentary inefficiency, but it may also actually rewire the brain toward less effective and more stress-reactive patterns.

Recognizing the value of focus is the first step – the next is to apply it in daily life. Here are a few practical strategies:

- *Deliberate monotasking.* Embracing the "one thing at a time" rule can radically transform your workday. For example, grouping similar tasks into dedicated blocks helps avoid constant context switching.
- *Digital hygiene and a supportive environment.* Silence mobile and email notifications during focus periods, close unnecessary apps or chats, and maintain a tidy workspace.
- *Mindfulness and restorative breaks.* Including mindfulness practices in your workday strengthens concentration while reducing stress.
- *Prioritization and learning to say "no".* Delegating secondary tasks is essential. Trust your team and offload responsibilities so you can focus on what only you can do.
- *A culture that values concentration.* Senior leadership should clearly communicate the value of neurofocusing. Some firms implement no-meeting days or "quiet hours" when everyone is expected to work on important projects without interruptions.

Once again, a single strategy won't save us, though it may improve circum-stances and bring greater peace of mind. The key is to build a system.

Defocusing – when we're "in the zone"

We've long believed that focus is good, and distraction is bad, simple as that. But neuroscience shows us that defocusing is instead a critical moment for creativity and problem-solving.

The ability to alternate between focused attention (Beta waves) and a more relaxed, diffuse awareness (Alpha waves) is essential for achieving sustained and creative concentration. When the brain enters an Alpha state, activity in the left prefrontal lobe decreases, and the default mode network (DMN) is activated. This network is associated with automatic processes and effortless thinking. It's during these moments – while showering, walking, or driving – that the famous "Eureka moments" often arise, the product of a relaxed mind making unconscious connections.

Alpha waves, especially when synchronized across the prefrontal and parietal lobes, help lower internal stress and muscle tension, expand perception, and grant access to previously acquired knowledge. This kind of open, effortless attention is critical in high-performance states, such as those experienced by elite athletes or deeply focused professionals, and is known as being "in the zone" – an optimal state where your best ideas, insights, and abilities flow with ease.

Neuroscience-based strategies

Time management depends on a variety of brain functions and key regions responsible for attention, planning, and decision-making. Incorporating strategies backed by neuroscience – such as setting clear goals, structuring the day using organizational techniques, practicing mindfulness, maintaining a consistent sleep routine, and breaking tasks into manageable steps – can make a significant difference in how we use our time.

Beyond improving productivity, these practices strengthen mental balance and contribute to a greater sense of wellbeing and personal achievement.

The two main enemies of time – perfectionism and procrastination

In addition to biological and attentional factors, there are two silent internal enemies of time management – perfectionism and procrastination. Both sabotage our performance from within – one disguised as high standards and the other as rest – but, in reality, they pull us away from focus, progress, and balance.

Perfectionism:
- Stems from the fear of not being enough.
- Steals time, energy, and mental peace.
- Can be overcome by retraining the brain – perfection isn't about doing everything flawlessly; rather, it's about doing it with purpose and enjoyment.

Procrastination:
- Is not laziness. It's an unconscious strategy to avoid emotional discomfort.
- Is driven by the limbic system's search for instant gratification (via dopamine).
- Is triggered by anxiety, fear, fatigue, or overwhelming tasks.

Perfectionism that multiplies the hours

Reviewing a document 20 times before sending it, making sure there isn't a single comma out of place, even though the content has been ready for hours. Postponing a presentation or article indefinitely because "It's not perfect yet" or "I don't have the exact wording", even though it's already more than adequate for its purpose. Refusing to delegate tasks because "No one will do it like I do", leading to overload and wasting time on things that could be shared. Overpreparing for a minor meeting or hearing, spending hours anticipating every possible objection or scenario, even if the actual impact of the meeting is low.

Sound familiar?

This behavior has a name – perfectionism. While it can be a valuable trait that pushes us toward excellence and high standards, it can also become a trap.

Perfectionism often arises as an unconscious response to the fear of not being enough, of not being accepted. It disguises itself as high standards or pursuit of excellence, but in truth, it's a silent force that never rests and doesn't let us rest either.

Those caught in a perfectionist mindset cannot simply "let things go" when they see something wrong. Even if they try, it feels impossible. It's a trait that may seem admirable from the outside, but if left unchecked, it can consume you from within. Unmanaged perfectionism wears you down. It drains your energy, peace, physical and mental health.

And the worst part? That all-too-common belief: "If it's not hard, it doesn't count. If I don't suffer for it, I don't deserve to be recognized or loved." As if value only lies in struggle, flawlessness, or exhaustion.

But there's another way to live – a gentler, freer one. The brain knows how to shine through flow, not just through control. When we release the need to do everything perfectly, we discover that what truly matters is not reaching an unattainable ideal but rather growing, learning, and enjoying the process.

Real perfection is not in the result, but in the authenticity with which we use our talents. Re-educating the brain to value the joy of development, instead of punishing ourselves for not having everything under control, is the real path to a more fulfilling life.

A far more powerful alternative is to replace the idea of perfection with that of continuous improvement. The difference lies in intention and emotional connection to the outcome.

Perfectionism is driven by fear – fear of making mistakes, of not meas-uring up, of not being enough. Its engine is anxiety, and its goal is an impossible ideal. The perfectionist doesn't enjoy the process, freezes at the possibility of failure, and rarely feels that their work is ever "good enough".

Continuous improvement, on the other hand, is born from learning and curiosity. It begins by accepting what's already done well, identifying what can be refined, and moving forward. It doesn't demand perfection; instead, it seeks progress. Continuous improvement is sustainable because it allows for mistakes, revisions, and growth. Perfectionism traps you; continuous improvement propels you. And while perfectionism creates constant tension in pursuit of the impossible, leading to distress and burnout, there's another major time management enemy that causes similar harm, but through a different path – avoidance.

Procrastination as a way to avoid immediate discomfort

Procrastination is not simply a sign of laziness or lack of discipline – it is deeply linked to how the brain manages stress, reward, and emotional discomfort. The brain naturally seeks to avoid immediate discomfort, whether emotional – like anxiety or fear of failure – or cognitive – like the overload caused by a complex task.

At the neurological level, procrastination results from a tension between two key brain systems – the prefrontal cortex and the limbic system.

The prefrontal cortex, located at the front of the brain, is responsible for executive functions such as planning, decision-making, and self-control. Its role is to guide us toward long-term goals. However, this region can be easily overpowered by the limbic system, a set of evolutionarily older brain structures responsible for regulating emotions and seeking immediate rewards.

When we face a task that triggers anxiety, doubt, boredom, or fear of failure, the limbic system activates and triggers an avoidance response. Instead of tackling the task, the brain seeks out distractions that offer instant gratification – checking your phone, snacking, scrolling through social media, or focusing on less important tasks. These activities, while irrelevant to our goals, trigger a quick release of dopamine, the neurotransmitter associated with pleasure, motivation, and, crucially, reward anticipation.

This process is doubly powerful – we not only feel relief from avoiding the uncomfortable task, but even thinking about the pleasant alternative can trigger a dopamine spike. This reinforces a negative feedback loop – every time we avoid a task, the temporary relief strengthens the link between avoidance and reward, making it more likely that we'll repeat the pattern in the future.

The amygdala, another limbic system structure, also plays a key role. In situations of perceived stress or threat (such as a deadline, presentation, or court hearing), it releases cortisol, the stress hormone, which intensifies the urge to avoid the source of discomfort. The longer a task is postponed, the stronger this avoidance impulse becomes, increasing anxiety and making action even harder.

Additionally, when the limbic system dominates, the brain tends to underestimate long-term consequences. In those moments, our perception of time becomes skewed toward the present – the immediate goal is to avoid discomfort now, while future consequences lose weight in our decision-making.

Breaking this pattern requires strengthening the executive function of the prefrontal cortex. Strategies such as meditation, mindfulness, setting small and specific goals, and cognitive restructuring – replacing automatic thoughts like "This is too much for me" with more functional ones like "I can handle it step by step" – can help restore the balance between emotion and intention.

Likewise, it's essential to develop greater tolerance for emotional discomfort, learning to face rather than avoid unpleasant tasks to disrupt the procrastination cycle.

In short, procrastination is a maladaptive emotional regulation mechanism, where the brain prioritizes short-term relief over long-term wellbeing. Understanding its neurological roots not only helps remove the moral judgment often associated with it, but also opens the door to more effective solutions, grounded in how the brain truly works.

By balancing the limbic system and the prefrontal cortex through strategies that strengthen executive function and reduce emotional reactivity, we can lower our tendency to procrastinate and improve our ability to face tasks proactively and efficiently.

Strategies to overcome procrastination

The challenge of overcoming procrastination lies in counteracting the powerful influence of dopamine and the limbic system.

- *Break down large tasks into smaller ones.* One effective strategy is to divide big, challenging tasks into smaller steps that offer more immediate rewards. This can trick the brain into releasing small doses of dopamine as each step is completed, helping maintain motivation and reduce the urge to procrastinate.
- *Establish reward systems.* Another useful technique is to connect task

completion with enjoyable activities, so the brain associates effort with gratification. The reward should be immediate and tangible to sustain motivation.

- *Automate.* Creating routines and habits that automate desired behaviors can help reduce the internal conflict between brain systems, allowing for more sustained focus on long-term goals.
- *Meditation and mindfulness.* Stress management techniques such as meditation and deep breathing exercises can reduce amygdala activation, which in turn lowers the fight-or-flight response that fuels procrastination.
- *The five-minute rule.* Commit to working on a task for just five minutes. This helps overcome the initial resistance and lowers psychological barriers. Often, once you start, motivation increases and you continue beyond the initial five minutes, as the brain has already crossed the procrastination threshold.
- *Pomodoro Technique.* Use the Pomodoro method – work in 25-minute intervals followed by short breaks. It's effective in maintaining focus and avoiding mental fatigue.
- *Create a low-friction environment.* Set up a workspace free from distractions by reducing environmental friction, which helps maintain focus and minimize temptation.
- *Practice self-compassion.* Procrastination is often linked to fear of failure or self-criticism. Practicing self-compassion means being kind to yourself when challenges arise, rather than engaging in harsh internal criticism. Reducing self-judgment also helps lower the anxiety that leads to avoidance.
- *Visualize.* Visualizing the benefits of completing a task and the steps to get there can boost motivation and clarity. A clear picture of the final goal and how to achieve it reduces uncertainty and increases willingness to start. Visualizing success can also strengthen self-belief and prepare the mind to face challenges, lowering anxiety and enhancing confidence.
- *Incorporate accountability.* Having someone to check in with or share your progress can be a powerful strategy against procrastination. The idea is that positive pressure from accountability encourages task completion and prevents avoidance.
- *The "5 Second Rule" by Mel Robbins.*[10] Counting down "5-4-3-2-1, GO!" creates a sense of control and conscious action. It activates the

prefrontal cortex, the brain's decision-making and self-control center. "Start before your brain kills the idea."

- *Next action technique.* David Allen's *Getting Things Done*[11] urges you to focus not on the final action, but the next actionable step. When a task feels vague, large, or undefined, the brain resists. The solution is to identify the smallest, most specific action you can take right now to move forward. For example, instead of writing "prepare report", write "open the document and review the first three paragraphs". This micro-clarity activates motivation and prevents paralysis.

Conclusion – mastering time starts with understanding your mind

In a world where technology pushes us toward 24/7 productivity, embracing neuroproductivity is no longer just an interesting option – it's an urgent necessity. We live surrounded by notifications, screens, constant interruptions, and a culture that values speed over quality, busyness over meaningful progress. In this context, neuroscience doesn't ask us to do more, but to do better, respecting the brain's rhythms, optimizing attention, and reconnecting with what truly matters.

Ignoring this perspective exposes us to two increasingly common traps – *toxic productivity* and *fake productivity*. While *toxic productivity* is the obsession with constant performance, glorifying exhaustion as a sign of success, leading to emotional and physical burnout, *fake productivity* is the illusion of progress – being constantly busy without moving forward on anything meaningful, caught up in minor tasks, multitasking, and urgencies that only create a superficial sense of efficiency.

Both have serious consequences – chronic stress, loss of focus, poor decision-making, and a growing disconnection from professional purpose.

Neuroproductivity, in contrast, offers a more human and sustainable compass for navigating time, the mind, and working with clarity, intelligence, and health.

References

1   Jorge E. Ovando, "Productividad y neurociencia", 2025, Neuroconoce®.
2   Michael Schladen, The Perception of Time, 2016, https://youtu.be/hwk7XbtjQso.
3   Ryan A. Wirt, Talha K. Soluoku, Ryan M. Ricci, Jeremy K. Seamans, James M. Hyman, "Temporal information in the anterior cingulate cortex relates to accumulated experiences", 2024, *Current Biology*.

4   Melina R. Uncapher, Monica K. Thieu and Anthony D. Wagner, *Media multitasking and memory: Differences in working memory and long-term memory*, https://link.springer.com/article/10.3758/s13423-015-0907-3

5   Ana Ibañez, *"Sorprende a tu mente"*, 2023, Planeta.

6   The Role of Mindfulness and Mental Health in Improving Employee Productivity, 2024, https://blogs.psico-smart.com/blog-the-role-of-mindfulness-and-mental-health-in-improving-employee-productivity-163481

7   Daniel Goleamn, *Focus: The Hidden Driver of Excellence*, 2015, Harper Paperbacks.

8   Mihály Csíkszentmihályi, *Flow: The Psychology of Optimal Experience*, 2008, Harper Perennial Modern Classics.

9   Innovative companies like Microsoft have reported a significant increase in team efficiency after implementing "no-meeting days" as they facilitate uninterrupted, high-quality workflow. Another inspiring example is Aetna, a major US insurance company. Its CEO, Mark Bertolini, introduced a corporate meditation and yoga program for employees aimed at helping them focus their minds and manage stress. The results were compelling – over 13,000 participating employees reported a 28 percent reduction in stress and gained an average of 62 extra minutes of productivity per week thanks to improved focus and calmness. Annually, this translated to approximately $3,000 in added value per employee, simply by improving their ability to concentrate and enhance wellbeing. Additionally, sleep quality improved by 20 percent, and participants reported reduced physical pain. Source: Luis Berdiñas, *Neurofocusing: el superpoder de la atención para líderes en la era de la distracción*, 2025, Infobae, www.infobae.com/opinion/2025/07/03/neurofocusing-el-superpoder-de-la-atencion-para-lideres-en-la-era-de-la-distraccion/

10 www.melrobbins.com/book/the-5-second-rule/

11 https://gettingthingsdone.com/

Chapter 10:
Make space for creativity – a path to wellbeing and peak performance

By Karen Dunn Skinner, co-founder, Gimbal Consulting

Making a change – any change – in how you work requires commitment. It takes effort. Even if you know that implementing the changes you're learning about throughout this book are going to help you manage your time better, it won't be easy. To keep yourself motivated when change gets tough, you need a really good reason. You need a "why".

In a recent presentation to an audience of 300 law firm owners, I shared why I protect my calendar so carefully, why I stay in my Power Zone and delegate as much as possible. It's so that I have time for three things – skiing in the winter, kayaking in the summer, and painting.

An audience member asked, "Why art? Shouldn't your 'why' be related to your business, not your personal life?"

My answer? Intentionally making space in my life for creativity makes me better at my business.

In a profession where your time is a commodity and your worth is based on the number of hours you bill and the rate you charge per hour, time spent on anything else is perceived as a waste. But is it?

What if creativity – any kind of creativity – unlocks even greater productivity? What if it makes you a better lawyer and a happier person? What if not working is what it takes to really practice at your peak?

Improving productivity with creative rest

Whenever I mention creativity to lawyers, the first thing I hear is, "I'm not artistic". But when I talk about creativity, I'm not talking about typically "artistic" endeavors. I paint, but that's just me. David, my work and life partner, cooks. Your creative outlet could be doodling, journaling, redecorating your house, or rebuilding that 1967 Chevy in your garage.

It doesn't matter *how* you're being creative. It doesn't matter that you haven't drawn more than a stick figure since you were 11 years old. It doesn't matter that you're objectively "good at it" or not. What matters is what those moments of creativity do for your brain.

In our time-focused profession, it can feel frivolous to carve out time for creativity. But this thinking rests on the false dichotomy that productivity and creativity are mutually exclusive. In reality, creativity doesn't detract from performance, it fuels it.

When you're working, your legal mind is always on – reading, negotiating, solving problems, anticipating risks, analyzing arguments. If you're running a practice, you're probably juggling business and administrative tasks as well. That sustained cognitive load is draining.

Studies show that when we engage in tasks that demand constant focus and decision-making, we experience what's called "ego depletion" – a drop in mental energy that leads to poorer performance over time.[1]

Processing vast amounts of information and multi-tasking, both inherent in the way we practice law, lead to cognitive overload and decision fatigue, further impacting performance. This isn't new. Research on cognitive load and exhaustion goes back decades.[2]

Making time for a creative activity of any kind allows your mind to recover from fatigue. This "creative rest" activates the prefrontal cortex, the seat of complex thinking and problem-solving. Neuroscientific research has shown that novel or creative tasks – like painting or improvising – can improve cognitive flexibility, pattern recognition, and the ability to make connections between unrelated ideas.[3] In other words, your legal problem-solving skills benefit directly from time spent being creative.

The power of small doses
"I'm too busy" is another common refrain when I suggest making time for creativity. But you don't need hours. Just a few minutes each day can give you the creative rest you need to boost your productivity.

Once a year, I set myself a 100-day art challenge. For 100 days (give or take – reality is never perfect!), I make time to put pencil or brush to paper. It could be five minutes or it could be an hour. Some days yield a full painting, others just a single layer, a sketch, or a color study. But no matter how long I spend, the results are consistent – I see a noticeable improvement in my focus, mood, and creative energy on the days when I paint. Over time, the act of showing up creatively – even briefly – becomes a source of restoration and resilience.

If a few minutes a day for 100 days sounds impossible, ask yourself this – do you spend five minutes every day doom-scrolling? I bet you do. In fact, it's probably more than five minutes (no one's judging, we all do it!). What if you spent that time differently? Start small. You don't have to commit to 100 days. For the next week, take those few minutes and do something creative – write in a journal, doodle on your legal pad, or whip up a batch of cookies with that new recipe you found.

These creative micro-breaks will give your mind a rest. Studies show that short, voluntary breaks taken throughout the workday involving creative or restful activity (as opposed to checking email or scrolling social media) lead to improved concentration, reduced fatigue, and better performance on subsequent tasks.[4] You don't need to allocate hours every day to feel the benefits of creativity.

Reframing creative time as strategic recharge is essential for high-performing professionals. Your mind needs space to wander in order to return sharper. The idea that "doing nothing" or "making art" is unproductive ignores the growing body of evidence that says otherwise, and feeds into the "busyness" culture of our profession. When you reframe creativity as a productivity tool, it might just be the one thing your practice is missing for peak performance.

Creativity as a stress-reduction strategy

In our office, there's a giant sticky note taped to the wall that says:

"We've never met an unhappy ex-lawyer."

It motivates us but, at the same time, it's heartbreaking. Behind that note is a truth we've seen over and over again. Too many lawyers feel trapped in careers that are draining the life out of them. This reality is what drives us in our coaching and consulting work and it's what has convinced me that our profession urgently needs more than time-saving tech or better billing practices. We need space – deliberate space – for the things that feed our souls.

Law is demanding. The emotional weight of legal practice is immense:
- Cognitive fatigue from non-stop decision-making and information processing.
- High-stakes pressure, where mistakes can cost clients, careers, or reputations.
- Perfectionism that leaves no room for error or experimentation.
- Vicarious trauma, especially for those in criminal, family, or immigration law, where you absorb your clients' pain.

Legal professionals consistently report low levels of wellbeing. A 2021 study by the Canadian Bar Association, the Federation of Law Societies of Canada, and the University of Sherbrooke found 57 percent of lawyers reported some level of psychological distress, compared with 40 percent for the overall working population in Canada during the same time period. For paralegals and notaries, it was over 65 percent and for articling students, it was a shocking 72 percent.[5]

Among all legal professionals, 28.6 percent reported suffering from depression, almost double the rate for the general population, while a whopping 35.7 percent reported anxiety, triple the rate of the general population.

A report by the American Bar Association and the Hazelden Betty Ford Foundation during the same time period found very similar results.[6]

Alarmingly, lawyers also score lower than the general population on resilience. Resilience is the psychological ability to bounce back from stress. Without resilience, stress easily becomes burnout.[7]

We need tools to build resilience, and one of the most powerful and under-utilized is creative expression. Unlike formal meditation (which doesn't work for everyone), creative practices provide an accessible and often more enjoyable form of mindfulness. Painting, writing, cooking, gardening, playing an instrument – these activities allow your brain to shift gears without shutting down.

Painting is one of the few things that brings me true mental stillness. My brain works quickly. There aren't many things that slow it down, but when I'm working with watercolor, I'm fully absorbed. I'm not thinking about work or worrying about the next deadline. I'm just watching the pigment move across the paper.

This kind of immersive, focused attention is what psychologist Mihály Csíkszentmihályi famously called "flow", a mental state in which people become fully engaged in a task that challenges them just enough to stretch, but not enough to overwhelm. Flow calms the mind, reduces anxiety, and builds emotional and cognitive resilience. It also gives the brain time to quietly process complex problems in the background.[8]

Sandra Behkor, another artist, lawyer, and consultant, uses intuitive art to process emotions before challenging moments. When she faces a difficult client conversation or a high-stakes presentation, she makes time for creativity. "Sometimes I can't name what I'm feeling", she says, "but when I sit down with a pen or brush, I can express it. I let it out on the page. And after that, I walk into the room with more clarity and strength."[9]

In a profession that leaves little room for error, creativity offers a safe place to let go. A place to feel, process, and heal. It's not just stress relief, it's restoration. And it's absolutely essential.

Increasing confidence with creativity

Perfection is expected of lawyers. We're hired to find problems, fix errors, and anticipate every possible outcome. Combine that with the relentless pressure to maintain a polished, unshakable image and you've got a culture where making mistakes, showing vulnerability, or admitting fatigue can feel like professional failure. But this version of confidence is brittle. It depends on performance, external validation, and constantly "keeping it together" even if you're falling apart.

Creative practice offers a different path to confidence – one rooted in self-acceptance and authenticity, not perfection.

When you sit down to make something – when you write, bake, or plant a garden – you reconnect with that part of yourself that exists outside your professional identity. You make decisions based on instinct and feeling. You express things without needing to explain them. You remember that you are a whole person, not just a "lawyer".

It can be very hard to let go of the perfectionism that's so ingrained in us. We all have an inner critic, a voice telling us our legal position is weak, our cake is too dry, or the cat in our painting looks like a turtle. But learning to let go in a creative context gives you confidence to let go professionally as well. It gives you strength to accept "less than perfect" and move on.

Sandra discovered this in a profound way after fracturing her dominant wrist. Unable to paint with her right hand, she began making art with her left. Something unexpected happened – the loud, relentless voice of her inner critic went quiet. "That voice didn't know what to make of the left-handed drawings", she explained. "Because I had no expectations of perfection, every-thing I made counted as art. And for the first time, I felt completely free."[10]

That freedom didn't stay in the sketchbook. It followed her into meetings, presentations, and difficult conversations. She began showing up with more confidence – not because she was perfect, but because she had silenced the inner voice.

I have a similar story. I am a perfectionist by nature. Working as a lawyer only reinforced this trait. As a painter, it's been hard to shake. At first, when-ever someone admired one of my paintings, I felt compelled to point out the flaws. "The perspective's off", I would say. "That color didn't come out right", or "It's not quite finished". Then a friend gently told me, "When you do that, you take away the other person's joy. They see beauty in what you've created. Don't make them unsee it."

Now, I practice saying something that once felt nearly impossible: "Thank you". No caveats. No self-deprecation. No explanations. Just appreciation. And that shift – to allow my work to be enough – is rippling into my professional life as well.

Whether you share your creative work or keep it entirely private, the act of creating helps you see yourself differently. You begin to value process over product. You build tolerance for failure. You learn to find satisfaction in small steps and tiny improvements. That's not just good for art, it's essential for leadership.

Creativity gives you a safe space to take risks, mess up, and still be proud of what you've made. It's where confidence is born. Not from being perfect, but for showing up anyway. For lawyers, that kind of confidence is revolutionary.

Achieving better outcomes for lawyers and clients

Lawyers are trained to spot risks, follow precedent, and find the flaw in any argument. These skills are essential for practicing law, but they're not the skills that drive innovation. They are not the skills that make us open to change and adaptable to powerful forces, like AI and legal technology, that are now impacting our profession.

Innovation and adaptation require something else entirely – the ability to see new patterns, imagine alternate paths, and connect seemingly unrelated ideas. That kind of thinking doesn't happen when your mind is stuck in problem-solving overdrive. It happens when you rest.

When you engage in a creative task that's absorbing but not demanding, like doodling, cooking, or gardening, you activate what neuroscientists call the default network. This is the same brain state associated with daydreaming, reflection, and subconscious processing. It's when your mind drifts and dips into the deeper layers of insight.[11]

Research shows that the brain continues to work on complex problems even when you're not consciously focused on them. This is called incubation, one of the core principles behind creative problem-solving.[12] That's why the advice to "sleep on it" is so effective, and why painting on it, baking on it, or planting on it can be just as powerful.

When you step away from a hard problem and shift into a restful, creative activity, your subconscious keeps working in the background. You allow your mind to reorganize information, make lateral connections, and generate unexpected solutions.

Creativity is especially valuable for lawyers because it breaks us out of the rigid mental grooves we often get stuck in. Legal thinking is deeply analytical. It's linear, rule-bound, and cautious. That's entirely appropriate for drafting contracts or arguing motions, but it doesn't help when you're trying to design a new service, reimagine how your practice operates, or develop a solution your client has never seen before.

You can't analyze your way to innovation. You have to create your way there.

Some of my best ideas for working through a coaching client's challenge, or for an article or a workshop, come to me in front of my easel, not my laptop. When you stop pushing and start playing, you allow insight to surface.

Conclusion

This is a book on time management, but you don't need hours of time set aside for a valuable creative practice. Creativity shouldn't be one more thing you need to manage. Start by taking a few minutes for yourself a few times a week. Write in your journal before bed. Doodle during a call. Weed a little patch of your garden. It all counts.

You also don't need to be good. People tell me, "I can't draw", "I'm not creative", "I'm so bad it's embarrassing". Stop. Being creative has nothing to do with being good. You're not trying to become a famous artist or world-renowned chef. You're already an excellent lawyer. This is about becoming even better by giving your brain time to recharge.

Our son is an emergency medicine physician. This year, he decided to learn the guitar. After a particularly hard shift, he sits down for a few minutes with his guitar and instructional videos. He loses himself in the notes. Is he good? No. Does he care? No. He's learning something completely new, creative, and entirely different. His guitar gives him flow. It recharges him. It fuels his soul.

You don't need lessons or expensive materials, either. Watch free videos. Use left-over school supplies, junk paper, and old notebooks. It doesn't matter. The point is not the result – it's the act of getting there.

As legal professionals, we rarely have total control of our schedules. A creative practice doesn't have to be daily to be effective. Allowing yourself short blocks of time to do things you already love, just for the joy of doing them, doesn't require perfection or a fixed schedule. And if you still struggle to "allow" yourself these moments, reframe them as recharge and value them as a productivity tool.

Creativity is not separate from your legal practice. It's not a luxury or an unproductive indulgence. Making time – even just five minutes a few times a week – can lead to improved wellbeing for you and better outcomes for your clients. It improves your focus, reduces your stress, and makes space for insight and clarity. It strengthens your sense of self and gives you energy to lead and serve others with greater impact.

The next time you feel stuck, the answer might not be in the next draft or spreadsheet. It might be waiting in your sketchbook. Or your kitchen. Or your garden. Sometimes the best legal thinking happens when you're not thinking like a lawyer at all.

References

1   Baumeister, R. F., Bratslavsky, E., Muraven, M., & Tice, D. M. (1998). "Ego depletion: Is the active self a limited resource?" *Journal of Personality and Social Psychology*, 74(5), 1252-1265. https://doi.org/10.1037/0022-3514.74.5.1252.

2   See, for example, Sweller, J. (1988). "Cognitive Load During Problem Solving: Effects on Learning." *Cognitive Science* 12(2), 257–285. https://onlinelibrary.wiley.com/doi/epdf/10.1207/s15516709cog1202_4.

3   Dietrich, A. (2004). "The Cognitive Neuroscience of Creativity." *Psychonomic Bulletin & Review*, 11(6), 1011–1026. https://doi.org/10.3758/BF03196731.

4   Albulescu P., Macsinga I., Rusu A., Sulea C., Bodnaru A., Tulbure B.T. (2022) "Give me a break!" A systematic review and meta-analysis on the efficacy of micro-breaks for increasing well-being and performance. PLoS ONE 17(8): e0272460. https://doi.org/10.1371/journal.pone.0272460.

5   Cadieux, N., Cadieux, J., Gouin, M.-M., Fournier, P.-L., Caya, O., Gingues, M., Pomerleau, M.-L., Morin, E., Camille, A. B.,Gahunzire, J. (2022). *Research report (preliminary version): Towards a Healthy and Sustainable Practice of Law in Canada, National Study on the Psychological Health Determinants of Legal Professionals in Canada, Phase I* (2020-2022). Université de Sherbrooke, Business School.

6   American Bar Association and Hazelden Betty Ford Foundation (2021). Well-Being Toolkit for Lawyers and Legal Employers. www.americanbar.org/groups/lawyer_assistance/well-being.

7   Dr Larry Richard has been researching personality traits in legal professionals since the 1990s. You can learn more and see his work here: www.lawyerbrain.com/.

8   Csíkszentmihályi, M., *Flow: The Psychology of Optimal Experience*. New York: Harper & Row, 1990.

9   Bekhor, S. (2025), in conversation with the author on Bekhor's podcast, *Get in the Driver's Seat*, Season 3, Episode 26, "Lawyers Need Creative Hobbies." www.youtube.com/watch?v=r5WFw74WI5g.

10   *Ibid.*

11   Andrews-Hanna, J., et al. (2010). "Evidence for the Default Network's Role in Spontaneous Cognition", *Journal of Neurophysiology* 104(1). https://journals.physiology.org/doi/full/10.1152/jn.00830.2009.

12   For a simple explanation of incubation, see: https://en.wikipedia.org/wiki/Incubation_(psychology).

Chapter 11:
Career planning and strategic time management

By Dr Todd Hutchison, global chair, International Institute of Legal Project Management

One of the greatest obstacles to identifying your career aspirations is the inability to get clarity on your ultimate desired role, and where you want your career pathway to take you. There are often too many options – from moving higher in your current organization's hierarchy through promotion, or towards aspirations in other work environments, such as external counsel, in-house counsel, juridical, academia, consultancy, or to simply change specializations.

As we start to progress our career, we shift from a young graduate with few to no skills and many choices, to having multiple skills with arguably fewer opportunities as we age. The time to get more serious about your career is when you realize that the important choices you make today are shaping where you end up tomorrow. You can plan for it to be great or put up with what others of influence allocate to you.

Take the analogy of a yacht in the ocean. You can wait to see where the current takes you, or you can grab the rudder, decide the amount of wind you need in the sails towards your envisaged direction, whilst still being able to shift and adapt to new weather conditions and changing routes.

The concept of career planning is to become clearer on your current view of your aspirations, developing a more structured pathway to achieve them. It establishes a career trajectory that reduces reactive decision-making and helps highlight professional development requirements, where more work experience or specialization is needed, and what strategic people networks you would benefit from. It is a method of accelerating your success to where you define it to be.

The intent is to ultimately have a greater purpose with rewards for your efforts in your chosen profession, and to seek roles that bring a sense of both contribution and accomplishment, whilst bringing value to those you serve. Whilst it does enable a roadmap, the strategy is not fixed, as it can be updated at any time. It is a starting point that allows you to investigate, explore, or trial new opportunities.

Statistically, you spend at least 23.8 percent of your week at work, and that contributes to 35.7 percent of your waking hours.[1] This means that your work is not only a large consumer of your time, but the money you make largely reflects the lifestyle options you enjoy during the other 64.3 percent awake hours.

In today's society, many people place great importance on a person's role and title as defining their identity and value. A law degree has always been a great foundation for many professions beyond legal practice, from academia to politics; however, it also offers many specializations and practice areas to choose from.

Individuals generally want different things, as not everyone has the ambition to become a partner of a firm, or to work full-time. The concept of a desired career pathway is defining what you feel is "success" for you and striving to achieve a work–life balance that brings satisfaction, as well as financial stability and rewards.

This chapter reflects on the different elements that may be worth contemplating when forming your career plan.

Balancing mental wellness into the plan

Modern legal practice is being impacted by artificial intelligence, and technology is progressing at a greater rate than ever before. This has added ambiguity and uncertainty to how it impacts current roles. As stress is a real or perceived loss of control, not understanding or welcoming the inevitable changes can place you in a state of flux, and career planning can help in feeling clearer and more confident in a pathway forward.

Legal culture has often glorified overwork that risks exhaustion, overwhelm, or even burnout. Sitting down and confirming how hard you want to play, and what elements in your life need to be changed, tweaked or adapted, all form a more strategic view of where you may want to realign yourself.

Your mental wellbeing should be a key factor when creating your career strategy, by determining how many hours, the level of responsibility, diversification, or specialization you want in your role, including how it supports your down time and non-work lifestyle.

It is not just about paid work – it is about having a sense of purpose, and that may come from pro bono work, getting more involved in professional associations and interest groups, or even seeking or providing mentorship. All of these can make you feel more connected, resilient, and refreshed.

Independent of where you are currently at, having a purposeful career and something to work towards can be healthy for the mind to feel renewed, to embrace new hope and find motivation. It can help make those hard decisions about changing your role or organization, as well as decisions like your retirement strategy.

Career planning through the lens of mental wellbeing can help you identify what work–life balance boundaries you may need, what life elements are not working for you, and how to reconnect with what you want to shift towards.

Portfolio careers bring diversity

The phrase "portfolio career" is being used to embrace multiple facets of a person's work that may comprise different roles, projects, or income streams, rather than working in a single job. This can include having various legal and even non-legal roles that combine to form a flexible, self-designed career structure.

A portfolio career generally needs to have a key income stream that is complimented with other roles, sometimes voluntary, that bring you more enjoyment, people connection, personal profile, awards, and recognition. This enables more resilience to market changes through income and skill diversity, and likely a greater purpose.

One outcome of the difficulties experienced during COVID-19 was the need to recognize flexible ways to work to generate income, and that some revenue diversity or having multiple income streams can better manage the future risks of such dramatic market impacts. Certainly, more people got to learn how to use online technology for virtual communications, and how it was to work from home.

The challenge is that strategic time management often becomes more critical when managing multiple roles. It is often accomplished by dividing your time, and sometimes the physical place of work, and managing your availability to specific days or times.

It is recommended that you create a list of any areas of interest, or options to further explore what would enhance your professional life, such as board roles, leadership roles, consulting assignments, coaching or mentoring, academic teaching, academic research, publishing, content creation, presenting, investing, mediation or arbitration, business development, legal project management, legal process improvement, technologist, defense reservist, advocate (lobbying or reform), side business activities, community pro bono contributions, or as a student for further education (e.g., LLM or PhD).

This concept can also be applied to transitioning times, such as maternity leave, returning to work from any break, building your own practice or side business, moving between different areas of law, changing roles, or reducing hours when transitioning to retirement.

A portfolio career in law is a shift from the traditional linear career path to a more dynamic, personalized and entrepreneurial approach to your career. It allows legal professionals to tailor their career pathways to their evolving interests, values, and lifestyle needs, whilst still contributing meaningfully to the legal ecosystem.

Behavioral profiling highlights your natural strengths

Psychometric tools have been a traditional way to help explore career options, or at least what natural talents a person may have that indicate the areas and tasks that best align to their core behavioral style.

The DISC model was created in 1928 by Dr William Moulton Marston in his book, *Emotions of Norman People*, and is used widely in assessing behavioral styles. Dr Marston defined DISC to represent four quadrants where a person can have one, two, or up to three behavioral strengths (compared to others) that constitutes their behavioral blend or dominating behavioral pattern. These are now commonly known as:

1. Dominant or driven that represent people who are ambitious and enjoy challenges and driving change.
2. Influencer that represent people who are highly social and enjoy people engagement opportunities.
3. Stable that represent people who like predictability and are happy to do repetitious tasks in their work.
4. Compliance that represent people who are intellectual-based, deep thinkers and like dealing with the details.

Behavioral traits are simplified by considering if a person's dominant style is more introvert or extrovert orientated, and task- or people-focused (see Figure 1). The D-style and S-style sit between the most introvert and most extrovert styles, and are more correctly known as an ambivert style.

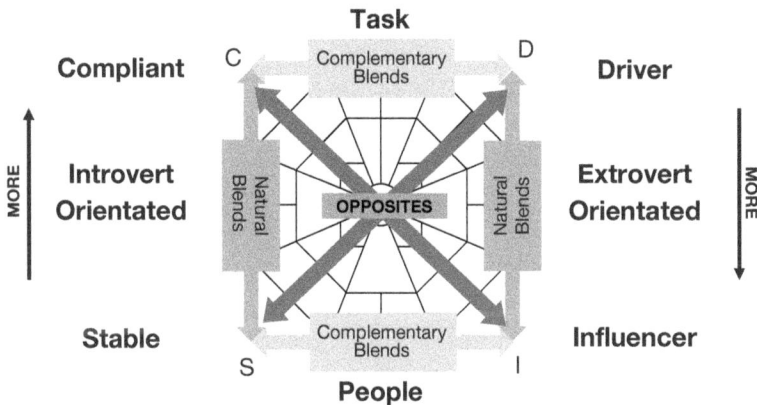

Figure 1: The four behavioral styles.

Although a person can have a behavioral blend that has aspects of opposite traits, they cannot play them at the same time. It is often said that "opposites attract" in relationships, and that is true on the grounds that the opposing traits bring balance to one another. This is also important when considering team formation, where opposing traits can bring greater synergy of skillsets.

Exploring your key traits is essential for career planning, as neuroscience suggests that when you are living to your natural talents, you are in "flow", where you do things easier, faster, and with more enjoyment. In these states you use the least energy so you can be most productive. It tells us what types of work are hard or easier for you as an individual – hinting at what roles you should be best aligned to, based on the typical dominating tasks they comprise. Although this is a complex area, and you undertake a behavioral profile to be able to rely on the information, the core generalizations about the traits and their main attributes will be briefly explained, limiting the information to each trait separately (remembering you have a behavioral blend that may include more than one).

D-style legal professionals
D-style legal professionals are typically competitive, decisive, and highly results-oriented. They prefer to move fast, take risks, and get things done as soon as practicable. They like to be in charge, have control and exert power, and – combined with being ambitious – generally want to be in a leadership role. They like change, think outside of the box, and enjoy challenges. The D-style lawyer will be keen to progress their career and ideally own or lead the legal practice.

They thrive on new, unique, innovative, or challenging legal matters. They are creative thinkers and can talk with confidence in the moment with little in-depth knowledge, yet sound convincing. They typically enjoy litigation work given their ability to talk on their feet, or other dynamic areas of law practice that provide interesting and non-repetitious work. They like exciting areas of law due to their sense of adventure and being unique. They typically have an entrepreneurial flair and are ambitious in pursuit of senior positions or even owning the legal practice.

When looking for roles with this trait, consider positions that:
- Have seniority (control);
- Require a results-driven approach;
- Have a sense of being fast paced; and
- Offer highly challenging or competitive opportunities.

When overdoing their strengths, D-style people can be seen by others as impatient, arrogant, overbearing, and exhibiting bullying behavior. They are often not very good listeners and are prone to making snap decisions, but are willing to change if shown a faster or better pathway to results.

I-style legal professionals

I-style legal professionals are typically talkative, sociable, optimistic, and lively. They are people-oriented, spontaneous, energetic, and enthusiastic. They tend to be positive and good at connecting and influencing others, and arguably come across as a friend to clients. The I-style lawyer will be able to attract work into the legal practice and take a lead business development role, as well as refer work to others. They are very good at promoting others and the organization.

I-style lawyers are usually good talkers and are able to get on well with most people. They typically excel in building and leveraging their relationships, and have a wide people network. They can be good at politics and building rapport fast with others. They are happy to attend events where they know no one and can easily engage in conversation. They present well, although prefer more generalized or high-level guidance when speaking. They are typically less detail-focus, so legal matters that rely heavily on people skills are best aligned to their strengths over very detailed legal tasks. They excel in networking and attracting clients to the practice, often taking up the business development function of the legal practice.

When looking for roles with this trait, consider positions that:
- Have a high level of people connection;

- Require refined interpersonal skills;
- Allow for testing the rules; and
- Include facilitation or presentation delivery.

When overdoing their strengths, I-style people can be inattentive to details, overly talkative, and emotionally driven. They may over-promise and under-deliver, as they are optimistic and are eager to be popular. Others may perceive I-styles as somewhat careless, impulsive, and lacking follow-up.

S-style legal professionals

S-style legal professionals are typically calm, helpful, modest, and predictable. They are eager to help, very loyal, and often make excellent team players. They tend to be good listeners, trustworthy, and seek to have purpose in helping others as they are very patient and persistent. They will be able to carry out the repetitious tasks typically required in many law disciplines. They are highly focused on fairness and justice, hence why many lawyers have this trait.

S-style lawyers tend to enjoy legal matters that have a purpose aligned to helping or serving others and are typically focused on fairness and equity (e.g., immigration and family law). They are customer service orientated, but do not need to be everyone's friend, as they prefer to work with fewer people and have deeper relationships. They are very intuitive. Trust is a critical factor to their relationships. They have good listening skills and people find them easy to talk to and happier to share information with.

When looking for roles with this trait, consider positions that:
- Provide a stable work environment with trusted people around them;
- Emphasize a social justice slant or a people-serving purpose;
- Require deeper connection with fewer people;
- Protect the under privileged; and
- Allow for predictability and repetitious tasks.

When overdoing their strengths, S-style people can be resistant to change as they need stability and security, or at least self-assurance to happily accept a change. They may be too willing to pitch in, overly compromising to meet everybody's requirements, and can be taken advantage of due to their supportive nature. Others may perceive S-style people as acting too slowly and being held back by comfort zones. The S style is people- and introvert-orientated.

C-style legal professionals

C-style legal practitioners are technical people. They are typically precise, logical, analytical, and careful in their actions. They need data and information and like to make informed decisions. They are focused on detailed tasks and ensuring things get done correctly, with an emphasis on compliance requirements. They produce quality work, have high standards, and mostly want to progress the work themselves (i.e., they find it hard to delegate).

C-style lawyers tend to enjoy the research elements of law and are deep thinkers. This is a very task-focused style, and they enjoy dealing with and overcoming difficult or complex issues. They like to stick with the rules and ensure a high level of compliance, often seeing things in black and white. They are adamant on what is right and wrong and don't like ambiguity. They generally go deep into the legal matter, enjoy the analysis work and any evidence-based investigation. They have an eye for risks, mistakes, and process deficiencies. They like to present information in the most accurate and correct way. They tend to enjoy working alone so they can focus on the detail and avoid distractions. They strive to be a specialist and don't like when they do not know something, hence are reluctant to speak when not able to be precise. They seek the information first to validate their thoughts.

When looking for roles with these traits, consider positions that:
- Enable them to work alone as a specialist;
- Require a high level of compliance;
- Require task and technical focus;
- Deal with detail and analysis; and
- Allow for adequate research time.

When overdoing their strengths, C-style people may focus too much on the details, becoming nit-picking and focused on the risks. At times, they get too involved in analysis and wanting to be correct. Others may perceive C-styles as being too critical, distant, pessimistic, and even cold.

Clarity and leverage are key

When determining a career pathway, it is often best to recognize that when you're doing things you love that are aligned to the areas that you're passionate about, and you're using your natural talents and experiences, you're likely to be in the best possible position for success.

There are two drivers to explore – "clarity" and "leverage". Clarity is summed up in the ongoing joke, *"I am still working out what I want to be when I grow up"*. Much of it is about not knowing what is out there that you would be interested in, or simply not knowing what you would be good at. This stops you identifying new opportunities.

Leverage is about seeking the clues that come from reflecting on the messages likely embedded in your past. Looking back at what you have done and reflecting on the relevance of these experiences can offer insights.

Consider the case study of a digital forensic specialist who started in the broadcast engineering industry, with his early career in commercial television and radio. He also previously worked in photography and studied music as the Conservatorium of Music. That gave him qualifications and experience in video, photography, and audio.

He was drawn to behavioral-based performance and was interested in human behavior, which led him to roles in security, law enforcement, and investigations, ultimately finding himself as a police musician (later becoming a Grade 2 world champion in pipe band music), a licensed security specialist, and investigator.

His core skills were in project management, ultimately merging his interests in law (as a law student at the time) to specialize in legal project management.

Legal project management recognizes that all legal matters are projects, which also extends to the fact that all investigation cases are projects. This leveraged his core project management skills.

When you merge the areas of law, law enforcement, project management, and investigation, it hints towards a career in forensics. Further study in that area led to a doctorate in forensics and legal project management. The missing piece was to have more relevant forensic-specific experience. By positioning himself to work with his mentor, Richard Boddington, who was a former chief detective inspector, intelligence officer, digital forensic specialist, and founder and principal of Forensics Australia, in joining forces, he became a recognized digital forensic specialist working in supreme courts across Australia.

The important aspect is that he accelerated his forensic career, working mainly in homicide and major crime, purely by specializing in multimedia-based digital forensics that solely focuses video, audio, and photographic evidence.

This role was an accumulation of his whole career background, which was never foreseen at the beginning of his journey and only spearheaded when he considered what he had done in the past that may hint to where he could position himself.

The person in question is me, in case you hadn't worked that out. It is now time for you to explore the same model I used to get your clarity and contemplate your leverage potential.

Getting your own clarity

To help you gain new insights from reflecting on yourself, your traits, and past and present experiences, you need to bring it all together to create an understanding of what you like to do, what you are passionate about, and your uniqueness that may enable the emergence of a pattern to highlight areas of career clarity or further exploration.

This model is an adaptation from the speaking profession, which helps speakers determine the topics best suited to craft their presentations and specializations. It has now morphed into the career options that may be highlighted by reflecting on your own life experiences and strengths and to get a new perspective on what you can leverage, and where it all may be heading.

It starts with creating three columns. The first column is where you detail all the activities and tasks you "like" or enjoy doing, which effectively represents the functions of a role you enjoy progressing (e.g., at the highest level: reading, writing, analyzing, speaking, mediating, mentoring, leading etc.). Your likes effectively highlight areas where work feels more like a calling, than a chore.

The second column is where the likes get context, by listing your "passions", which represent the topics you find of interest. If you put "Reading" in column one, column two explores what topics you like to read about. Passion fuels purpose and helps you persist through challenges, often getting consumed when learning more about them. It is not necessarily the life passions that you leap out of bed for – rather, things of great interest that grab your attention.

The third column defines your uniqueness or "differentiation" between you and others. Sometimes you have to seek other people's opinion to understand what they believe your natural gifts and talents are, because they are often hard for you to identify yourself. Think of the things that people come to you for, as they see them as something you do very well. For example, you might be multilingual, you may have worked in the private sector or government, in a law firm or as in-house counsel. You may have worked nationally and internationally, or you might have specific qualifications and training. These are all things that allow you to identify how you are different to other people.

Once you have created these three lists, it is important that you use the process of "chunking", which takes broad statements down to the right level of detail to gain meaningful insights. Chunking is a term used in psychology for going down to a deeper level of detail. For example, if considering "transport", you would chunk down to the many transport types from cars, motorbikes, trains, planes etc. If you then chunk down for a car category, you would identify the types of vehicles, such as sedan, station wagon, SUV, limousine etc. Then if you keep chunking down the information, you ultimately get to a make and model of car. Chunking effectively allows you to get down to the detail needed to be at a meaningful level of insight to your thinking, remembering the adage, *"The devil is in the detail"*. This is a straightforward process, but not necessarily easy to do. It can take time to chunk down to the right level, but the insights can give you much more clarity as to the career options you should explore.

Once you have chunked down to the maximum level of detail possible and you have these three lists well populated, you then use a colored pen and start joining items that are related. For example, you may have had "training" as an activity you enjoy (like); however, you only enjoy educating people in "dispute resolution" (passion). Then you connect it to the fact that you may be an accredited mediator, and other mediator-type experiences you have had (uniqueness). The color should disclose a "theme".

You then get a different color pen and connect the next related items, potentially highlighting another theme (you usually have different facets to yourself that could take you down different career pathways or professions).

When you finally finish color marking the related items with connecting lines, you may find when you step back that there is one or more dominant colors that represent major themes that could hint to what you should be leveraging. Effectively it will provide the key elements that could suggest a specific role to pursue that makes the most of them.

It works because it follows the premise that if you love what you're doing, you're passionate about it, and you're leveraging all your uniqueness and natural talents, then you're likely living a life where work will be more enjoyable, and where you are doing things faster, more effectively, and with the least energy. This likely aligns with your core behavioral style.

This will then allow you to consider what roles you can explore or focus on to determine the most likely pathway your career should take. If you have too many options, prioritize them, or start eliminating the ones that don't interest you the most. You may end up with more than one role, and it may be that this provides insights to adopting a portfolio career option.

The last part of the exercise is to consider whether the role(s) has the appropriate pay and rewards, and offers a clear market to those who need these services or function. Income does have a major impact on you and your family's lifestyle and therefore is an important decision factor.

Strategic time management

Once your career plan has identified your ideal career position, you can start with the next clear role to focus on. You can carry out career planning in stages, one role at a time. If you know your end position clearly and all the dependent roles before it, then you have your career progression strategy, and each role you have on your career pathway can be listed. Now the real strategy is required.

The concept of "strategic time management" is the deliberate and goal-aligned use of your time that encompasses scheduling activities and tasks and setting achievement dates for your professional development, personal positioning, strategic relationships, and role-aligned experience actions.

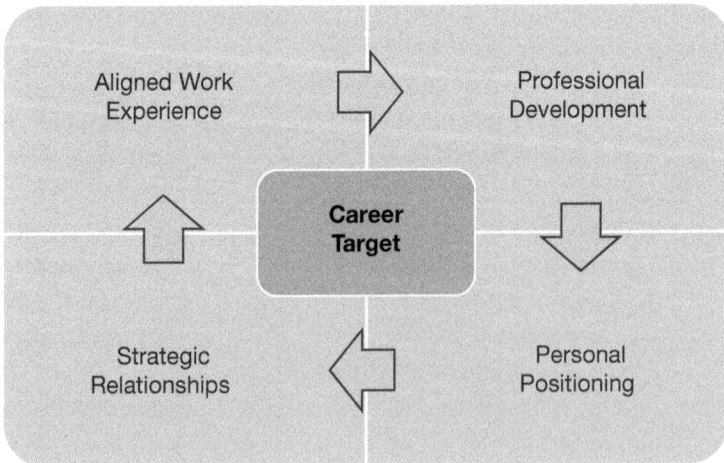

Figure 2: A targeted career plan.

Strategic time management is best considered when you have your final destination role in mind. However, you may need to go into other roles first that are prerequisites. This is the concept of a career pathway. Take the example of a student aspiring to be a judge. This typically requires them to complete a law degree, become licensed to practice law, complete the barrister exam, and gain aligned experience. When you determine the end goal, it is easier to then step back and examine the pathway from where you currently are to that destination point.

It is also smart to analyze people who are already in your aspiring role and see what qualifications, attributes, networks, memberships, and experiences they have, with consideration to any prerequisite or desired skills and experience outlined in job descriptions. It may also serve you to connect with those people and ask more questions about the role and how they got there.

In summary, the element of time is not just about getting things done – it's about getting the right things done to move your career forward. It is also about putting a schedule in place to define specific goals, such as completing specific training courses, as you progress. Without adding dates to focus on, you will not get started as it will all fall into the "one day" basket that never arrives. Goals work most effectively when you have goalposts to work towards.

Professional development

Maintaining the profession's continuous professional development (CPD) points offers a good reason to start better defining your educational needs that will serve you. Any training in legal process improvement, legal project management, and artificial intelligence applications in law will always be beneficial. However, you can start by being more selective in aligning training opportunities to the knowledge and skills required for your career path.

Make a list of any knowledge and skills gaps you have for identifying suitable short courses, and consider any further qualifications, certifications, permits, licenses, or exams that may be warranted to meet the prerequisites of your future role. Doing these often highlights to others your interests and direction. For example, the action of a person enrolling in a Master of Business Administration (MBA) suggests they have an intent to be moving into, or growing in, a leadership role.

It is now about being more strategic with your development time and preparing yourself for your future direction.

Personal positioning

Not all legal professionals are interested in having a high profile – however, having a personal profile does lead to more opportunities and support from others. Where a lawyer can attract more work, they become more valuable to the firm, and therefore being known has many benefits.

Although the saying goes, *"It is not what you know, it is who you know"*, this statement is not completely true. It is important to know people; however, if you are not competent when they link you to an opportunity that does not achieve good results, they will never refer you again. You must be good at what you do – always.

More important is the adage, *"People prefer to do business with people they know, like, and trust". The keyword in this statement is "know".* This is because you must know the person to be able to even have the opportunity of trusting and liking them.

The most interesting insight is that you can be known through many different mechanisms without having actually met anybody. This may include being an author, a board director, speaker, award winner, appearing on social media, appearing in interviews, or podcasts. These are all profiling positions where you get personal exposure, without the reader, attendee, or listener having met you personally. If they like what you say, they will generally like and trust you. This means the opportunities to build your profile and expertise are wide ranging when you are more strategic at where you turn up. If you attend a presentation as an attendee, you will only get to know a few people. As the presenter, the whole room will suddenly know you. This is the differentiator of strategic time management – you have accelerated your profile beyond having to have met them in person.

Social media platforms, such as LinkedIn, provide free opportunities to publish articles, and if done strategically they can be structured to emphasize your knowledge in a specific specialist area – effectively leading to recognition of your expertise. This could lead to you being seen as the expert on a particular topic, or at least a person others may want to engage or employ. This extends to writing articles for professional association-based magazines that are always looking for contributions. You simply need to write an article and ensure it finds its way to the appropriate editor.

Many extrovert lawyers are already well-known, liked, and trusted. However, they haven't explained what exactly they do. If a listener doesn't know what you do, it's impossible to actually refer or engage you. This extends to how you introduce yourself when you meet people. It is called the "elevator speech" due to the concept that, in an elevator, you have limited time to introduce yourself. It therefore needs to be short and clear. It aims to let the person know what you do as a profession and ideally how this helps them and others.

Determining how you introduce yourself can be one of the most effective ways to identify and refine who you are, and what value you bring. If the message is clear, you have clarity as to what you do, and what you offer as value for others to engage with.

Many people introduce themselves as a lawyer. However, that isn't enough – you need to tell them the practice area and what value you can bring them or others they may know. For example, *"My name is Todd and I am an intellectual property attorney. I help innovators, creators, and business owners to protect the value of their ideas – whether it's a brand, invention, design, or digital content. From securing patents and trademarks to managing licensing and resolving disputes, I make sure your intellectual assets are legally safeguarded and commercially optimized."*

Drafting and memorizing an elevator speech can make you clearer about your value too. Clarity is key in explaining what you do and how you can help others, and this knowledge can lead to an engagement or referral.

Strategic relationships

Once you have your current position clear, as well as your intended career goals, strategic relationships can accelerate your pathway to success. Career-building doesn't happen in isolation, and other people are the ones who promote, approve, or refer you. The climbing of the career ladder requires the support of others.

Consider the case study of an adjunct associate professor seeking promotion to professor level. He was well published, he had attracted research grants, progressed amazing initiatives, and participated in national and international initiatives. The challenge was that his work and profile was not so well-known in his own university. Professorial positions are limited by number, so without having strategically built his profile and connecting with the promotional committee, he could be overlooked, solely from focusing on doing the right things, but neglecting to build the right internal relationships.

In contrast, consider the case where a PMI member became the president of the local chapter, which led to the other local chapters knowing them, leading to an election to become the first independent national chairman. In that role, they became known by other nations, to become the first elected global board director from their nation. They were not focused on building their personal profile – it was a consequence of their strategic positioning.

Many lawyers are introverts, and the idea of building strategic relationships may be off-putting. However, the following behavioral trait-based opportunities may highlight options that achieve the same or similar outcomes for each behavioral style that may be used to consider a few of your own options.

D-style legal professionals (extrovert orientated) could consider:
- Board positions.
- Speaking at events.
- Strategically aligned short-term pro bono assignments.
- Interviewing others in their area of interest.
- Social media contributions (statements, articles, videos, photos, podcasts etc.).
- Strategic awards and recognitions for their initiatives.

I-style legal professionals (extrovert) could consider:
- Strategic networking events.
- Speaking at events.
- Strategic pro bono assignments where a lot of people are involved.
- Cold calling or contacting strangers by phone or email.
- Interviewing others.
- Mentoring programs.
- Educational institute lecturing.
- Social media contributions (statements, articles, videos, photos, podcasts etc.).

S-style legal professionals (introvert orientated) could consider:
- Pro bono assignments.
- Board of management positions.
- Mentoring programs.
- Educational institute lecturing.
- Social media contributions (statements, articles, videos, photos, podcasts etc.).
- One-on-one informal meetings.

C-style legal professionals (introvert) could consider:
- Publishing as a researcher or specialist.
- Pro bono assignments requiring technical expertise.

- Board of management positions in more compliance or expert functions.
- Speaking at technical events where they know the topic well as a specialist.
- Educational institute lecturing requiring high technical expertise.
- Professional association committee roles in more compliance or expert functions.

Professional associations are a great place to meet and reconnect with people. They usually run a monthly meeting that includes content delivered by a speaker and networking time. Relationships that are nurtured over time often bring great benefits.

When you are not in your desired job, you are recommended to connect with people who are, as they have the knowledge about the role, its requirements, and what you may need to be eligible. They are also often the first to hear about any vacancies or opportunities that may come up. As they are doing, or have done, what you aspire to do, they are in an ideal "mentor" position for you.

Strategic relationships are a fundamental way of building useful connections with key people that may promote, refer, and work with you in the future. It is not only about connecting with the right people, but delivering value in your exchanges with them.

Aligned work experience

Sometimes, roles call for previous or related experience that you may not yet have. This is where strategic relationships can sometimes be leveraged to open the door. Otherwise, you will need to demonstrate other methods to get enough experience to meet the requirement. You could utilize your next annual leave period to undertake work experience, offer to do project-based assignments after-hours, seek a secondment, or take on part-time related work.

There may be other ways of getting exposure to the industry through working on professional association projects or sitting on boards in the same field. Undertaking further study in that area or utilizing the article-writing route may also help demonstrate your knowledge and interest as a method of getting noticed, and that may be deemed enough to get you the opportunity.

It is simply about demonstrating your willingness and desire for that role, and leveraging your past background and people networks to get a foot in the door. You have to create a workable strategy and be persistent. There have been times that jobs have specified a certain qualification as a mandated requirement, yet they have accepted candidates who were enrolled and still completing it. At the end of the day, employers want to engage people who genuinely desire the role and want to perform in it.

Last thoughts

Career planning is not a one-off plan, particularly given the activities discussed. It is something that needs to be reviewed, lessons learnt, reflected on, and updated further as you get more clarity or when circumstances change. Guiding your yacht requires considering the wind, the storms, the speed, the depth of water, the current, and the obstacles in your path. This means frequent adjustments, planning for the unknown, but enjoying the journey to the destination. When you achieve it, it will feel like a greater accomplishment as you can appreciate the pathway you endured to get there.

Career success in the legal profession rarely happens by accident. Intentional career planning and strategically managing your time to develop and position yourself can help guide you to a rewarding, sustainable, and influential career. Whether you are just starting out or have decades of experience, take the time to reflect, dream, and make decisions as to where you want to position yourself in the ever-evolving legal profession and beyond.

Reference

1   Based on a 40-hour week and 56 hours (eight hours per night) of sleep per week.

Chapter 12:
Mastering time for a successful legal career

By Rachel Brushfield, The Talent Liberator™® and founder of EnergiseLegal

Why are lawyers so time pressured?

A lawyer's role is about solving problems. In private practice especially, work can be intense. Often, clients delay sharing problems, but want them solved yesterday, and to not pay too much. This is pressure – dealing with tricky cases or deals, under the scrutiny of time codes, and with increased competition, while embracing increasing automation and AI. Lawyers in private practice are given fee earning targets and used to be measured in six-minute units of time. Some still are, which increases the pressure. Time recording is pressure in itself – accounting for how you spend your time every single day.

Pressure and tight deadlines do not enable headspace – necessary to take a step back for yourself and think about your own career. This is magnified if you manage a team, have children, are a carer for aging parents, own your own firm, or are responsible for getting your own clients as a consultant lawyer. Certain practice areas can be very intense, including corporate and commercial deals. Seasonality in certain specialisms can be full-on for a few weeks or months (for example, divorce for family lawyers in January each year and the end of the financial year for private client lawyers).

This is why it is so important to make career planning in your head and in your diary equally as important as fee earning.

How to free up time in the working day

There are a number of ways to free up time in the working day.

- *Prioritization* – become skilled at prioritizing important and urgent tasks.
- *Delegate* – give tasks to junior members of the team so you free up time for strategic matters and career planning.
- *Marginal time* – use commuting time to listen to podcasts. When queuing face-to-face or on the phone, use this time smartly so it isn't dead/wasted time.

- *Say no* – get skilled at saying no comfortably so that you don't lose precious time.
- *Avoid "time frittering"* – become aware of how you fritter away time, for example mindless scrolling on your phone, browsing online shopping sites, etc. These are displacement activities that prevent you from focusing on what you really need to be doing.
- *Audit time use* – keep a diary of how you spend your time to identify insights. Creating a pie chart of different tasks, thinking about what would be your ideal time split in future, and then what needs to change to enable this change is very beneficial.
- *Time block* – plan ahead and block out time for career planning regularly, so that you know it is scheduled into your working week.
- *Take breaks* – taking regular breaks helps to re-energize and maintain your productivity and prevent burn-out.
- *Collaboration and support* – tap into others' expertise. Don't be afraid to ask for help – it is wise, not weak. Different people have different strengths – it makes sense to play to your strengths.
- *Employer resources* – utilize any career resources provided by your employer. Larger companies may have a subscription to an online career management service, personality testing, have a mentoring or sponsorship scheme, or pay for you to have a coach.
- *Set reminders* – use your phone to set reminders for certain tasks, e.g. a quarterly review of achievements and initiatives, creating new case studies of cases or deals that you have worked on.
- *Diarize reflection* – regular focused and purposeful reflection is very beneficial in a fast-paced job, for example half an hour a week on a Friday.
- *Time code* – give career planning a time code to give legitimacy to it in your mind.
- *Accountability buddy* – whether a friend, colleague, career coach, or mentor, it can help to "check in with them" to stay on track.
- *Utilize tech and apps* – these can automate meeting bookings and block out time for focused work. Some automatically reschedule meetings and provide analytics on time usage.
- *Utilize career networks* – for example Law Careers, which has resources for solicitors and barristers.[1]
- *Understand procrastination* – it is the thief of time. Lawyers are perfectionists so this magnifies the likeliness of procrastination happening, reducing the amount of time you have. Causes of procrastination are

complex and multifaceted, so understanding your own causes can liberate a lot of lost time.

The importance of taking time to plan your career

Career planning is primarily an important but not urgent task, so easy to postpone. If you have been made redundant, it becomes both an important and urgent task. Solicitors are notoriously busy, so making time to plan your career can be a challenge. Giving career planning a project name is a good idea so that when you look at it in your diary, it feels important and motivating to do. Lawyers need to feel purposeful. Creating a checklist and breaking the task down into bite-size tasks, with a time estimate by each and putting them in your diary, makes career planning realistic and doable, rather than overwhelming.

A checklist for your career planning might include these items:
- Craft compelling SMART short- and long-term career goals.
- Create a plan to achieve your career goal.
- Block out time each week for career planning and purposeful analysis and reflection.
- Start a reflection journal – experience, knowledge, and skills.
- Look at world of work trends.
- Analyze competitors.
- Review and update your LinkedIn profile.
- Speak with a supportive recruiter/head-hunter who "gets you".
- Look at the Law Society website for free career resources.
- Research webinars and conferences.
- Review your personal brand.
- Research experienced career coaches with deep understanding of solicitors and the legal profession.
- Do an up-to-date SWOT (Internal Strengths and Weaknesses, External Opportunities and Threats) analysis.
- Do an up-to-date PESTLE (Political, Economic, Social, Technological, Legal and Environmental) factors analysis.
- Ask colleagues for feedback about your strengths and development areas.
- Define up to date career capital SMART goals – what makes you marketable.
- Review and set new CPD (Continuous Personal and Professional Development) SMART goals.

- Build and grow your face-to-face and online networks.
- Update key words for your legal specialism.
- Create a content plan for LinkedIn.
- Define your career purpose.
- Write a list of questions for which you want the answers.
- Record career achievements and write case studies for deals/cases that you have worked on.
- Ask for testimonials and recommendations on LinkedIn.
- Write what you would like to be written about you in *Legal 500* and *Chambers*.
- Plan a career planning and review away day, turning off all notifications to avoid being distracted from deep thinking.

You could delegate this task completely to a virtual PA or try AI for some of them – for example, ask Perplexity or ChatGPT a "prompt", e.g. "What legal skills will be in demand in 2030?".

The benefits of making time to plan your career accrue over time. The opportunity cost of failure to make time means you can be left behind by your competitors for prized jobs – they on the front foot and you on the back.

In uncertain times, it is especially important to create a future-proof career. We live in a VUCA (Volatile, Uncertain, Complex, and Ambiguous) world and you need to have career plans 'A', 'B', and 'C'. Do you?

Make time to be clear about these career options. Start today.

Practical examples of how to make time to plan your career

Different people like career planning in different ways. Some people like to talk it through, others prefer support and working with an expert face-to-face, e.g. a career coach or mentor, while others like to self-reflect using books and a workbook. Others like to work in a group and share ideas and experiences, e.g. on a webinar, workshop or career retreat. Some prefer online coaching as it is easier to fit in their schedules. Some like structured learning, e.g. a 12-week course to work through, broken down into sections. Others like to listen to podcasts and watch videos. What is your preferred learning style?

How do you like to career plan? Thinking about how you learn will mean that it is more likely to happen. I find that a day trip on a quiet train works really well to think, focus, and reflect. I come back to my office with a renewed sense of purpose, feeling energized.

Having a clear 12-month cycle that works for you is important too – the calendar year January to December, financial year April to March, or a year starting with your birthday.

The Law Society[2] in the UK has a comprehensive careers advice section on its website free to members. It also plans career events every year, for example, moving in-house, becoming a consultant lawyer etc., as well as career case studies for a variety of lawyers. A lot of the events are online and are also recorded, so that you can listen to them at a time to suit you and your schedule.

My book for the Law Society, *Career Management for Lawyers. Practical strategies to plan your next chapter*,[3] also has useful exercises and tips.

LinkedIn learning,[4] becoming an alumnus of your law school, WhatsApp groups (e.g. senior women working in-house), the newsletters of various experts, the Crafty Counsel network for In-House lawyers, the specific sections and communities of the Law Society (Women Lawyers, Junior Lawyers, In-house, Disabled, Small Firms, LGBTQ, etc.)[5] all have useful resources. Setting up Google alerts is an expedient way of gathering information, as is following individuals and firms on LinkedIn. There is a plethora of information out there!

Joining a high-quality paid membership network such as Winmark Global or Managing Partners Forum may also provide access to useful content, data and networks very relevant to you to learn from. There are many specialist networks for different stages of a legal career, so tap into your own network to help you to find them.

Strategic tools and frameworks for career planning
There are many strategic tools that are practical and insightful to help you plan your career. My career heritage was in marketing and brand strategy and communications, so these are second nature to me. I use quite a few self-completion questionnaires with my career coaching clients because they are quick to do, identify priorities, and help inform what coaching they need, so create expediency.

Some people like analytical tools, other people reflective, and others experiential.

SWOT analysis
A SWOT analysis is a useful framework for synthesizing information following analysis. It is typically a two-by-two matrix that you fill in with points for each heading.

Internal – strengths and weaknesses (you).

- Strengths – your strengths.
- Weaknesses – areas that you need to improve to make you more marketable.

External – opportunities and threats (the market).

- Opportunities – external emerging jobs and skills e.g., cyber, green/the environment.
- Threats – things that may have a detrimental impact on your career prospects and aspirations. For example, there is currently a lot of media coverage in the UK about the impact of AI on lawyers' jobs, employers not increasing headcount because of increased Employer National Insurance (NI), and a general trend to "younger, leaner, cheaper".

PESTLE analysis model

The PESTLE analysis model gets you to think broadly about the different factors that may impact on your future career.

- *P = Political factors* – government, trade and tax policies, general political issues, changes in leadership, regulation, and political trends.
- *E = Economic factors* – inflation, interest rates, exchange rates, economic growth, and unemployment levels.
- *S = Social factors* – cultural trends and patterns in society such as lifestyle trends, age distribution, and consumer behavior.
- *T = Technological factors* – technological advancements and developments, innovations, scientific advancements, and economic breakthroughs.
- *L = Legal factors* – labor and consumer laws, market and import/export regulation, health and safety policies and guidelines.
- *E = Environmental factors* – climate change, environmental regulation, waste management policies, and consumer environmental awareness.

Ansoff's Matrix

Ansoff is a framework used in innovation to help you to *"think outside of the box"*. I have adapted it for the career planning context.

It gets you to reflect on current skills and new skills, and current markets and new markets, and the potential connections between these. It is a useful framework to help you identify new career opportunities that might appeal to you to pivot into, from evolutionary to revolutionary. It is typically a two-by-two matrix.

Four-step strategic review framework

This is a useful and intuitive exercise that is quick to do and creates instant insights and clarity. If you are feeling overwhelmed and stuck, it is a useful starting point. You can then reflect on what emerges and then work out the next steps.

1. Where am I and why am I there?
2. Where could I be?
3. How could I get there?
4. How will I know that I have achieved what I set out to do?

Personality tests

Personality tests can provide useful insights. I have found Myers Briggs, Belbin, DISC, and Talent Dynamics all enable different insights to help you plan your career.

Try different strategic tools – there is no right or wrong. What is right is what works for you.

Creating a bespoke tool or exercise can be very useful too – this is something I relish doing with my clients!

Career scenario planning

Career scenario planning is a strategic process where individuals map out several possible future career paths based on various internal and external factors, such as personal aspirations, market trends, industry changes, and life circumstances.

Originating as a business tool, scenario planning is increasingly used for personal and career development, especially in professions subject to rapid changes and competition, like law.

Career scenario planning involves looking at different scenarios in your career, the best-case scenario, the worst-case scenario, and everything in between, giving a thorough and balanced perspective about the future based on analysis and synthesis.

The process includes looking at both internal factors and external factors. It helps individuals to map out different possible career paths based on various internal and external factors, e.g. personal aspirations, market trends, profession changes, and life stage circumstances, such as the need to look after school-age children or fund your children through university.

Internal factors include looking at goals, strengths and weaknesses, motivations, and personal values.

External factors might include researching market trends, industry disruptions, and workplace evolutions, such as AI replacing some legal roles previously done by lawyers and the automation of various repetitive legal tasks, negating the need for a human to do it. Scenarios for different legal roles would be developed, for example, moving in-house, pursuing the partnership track in private practice, developing a portfolio career, becoming a consultant lawyer, or changing direction out of the law to do something completely different, developing one or more side gigs to broaden out future career options.

Action steps, skills development requirements, and decision points become clear for each career scenario, giving peace of mind in an uncertain world from a thorough, rigorous, and robust process.

The benefits to solicitors of career scenario planning include:

- Preparing for uncertainty.
- Making better informed career decisions based on fact and analysis, not hope and wishful thinking.
- Skills and network development.
- Developing transferable skills.
- Importantly for solicitors who worry a lot, reducing anxiety from a thorough and robust process.

It is important to review different career scenarios, especially in a fast changing and uncertain world. This helps to create career agility and the ability to pivot in different directions should the need arise – your career plan 'A', 'B', and 'C', so that you are on the front foot, not the back. It helps to detail the implications of career decisions, such as specializing in a specific niche, retraining, studying for a further legal or non-legal qualification, or moving firms as a lateral partner.

In a nutshell, career scenario planning helps solicitors navigate a complex and evolving professional landscape, increasing confidence and control over their career direction, reducing fear of the unknown and the risk of burnout.

As part of this chapter I spoke to two inspiring lawyers about their career trajectories and how they made time to plan where they wanted to be.

Penny Rinta-Suksi, commercial partner at Blake Morgan

How did you become a lawyer?

"I enjoyed law and followed the educational and career path into it, discovering what I enjoyed most as I went along."

What role did mentors and coaches play in your career planning?

"They played a huge role. Mentors helped me to focus and plan and think more strategically. Coaches helped me to understand my values, prioritize, and make the right decisions with my career."

Who inspired your career?

"My father put the idea in my head. TV shows like *LA Law* and *Ally McBeal* helped me on my way! My jujitsu teacher helped me to get the legal 'bug'."

How did you create time and space to plan your career?

"My most significant career changes have taken place at milestones. Once I qualified as a solicitor, I knew I was not ready to settle down and spent two years working abroad as a legal consultant. After that break, I knew I was ready to take on more and became a partner within six years. Immediately before my current role, the market shifted and I found myself in a perfect moment to take a more strategic look at my career with a career coach. This proved to be invaluable and has helped me get to the position I am in today. I feel as though I am in my perfect job with time for myself, my family, and my hobbies as well."

What advice would you give to young lawyers at the start of their career about career planning?

"Initially, you should do what you enjoy and increase your experiences and exposure to different types of work so that you can figure out what it is that sets you alight! After that, be more strategic about how you can get more of the type of work that you want to do. If you want to be promoted, you need to behave like you have already achieved the role that you want to achieve. To be an owner in a business you need to think like an owner in the business. A business case to prove your value and worth is a key requisite for any phase of your career, especially prior to promotion."

Looking back at your career, what do you wish you had done differently?

"I wish I had 'backed myself' more. I took criticism deeply to heart. This helped me to become a better lawyer, but it also meant a number of very low points. A mentor, coach, or support network at those times in my junior career would've been very helpful."

What are your top three tips to plan your career?

- Do what you love.
- Be strategic and have a plan.
- Have a coach or mentor you can trust.

Anything else that you want to add?

"Nothing will change unless you take action!"

Maria Madara, associate at KaurMaxwell, a female led-and owned boutique full-service law firm in London founded by Mandeep Kaur Virdee while she was eight months pregnant

How did you become a lawyer?

"Law was always my chosen career path, but I knew from the outset that I wanted to build a broad base of experience before committing fully to it. I began my career working for Senate Majority Leader Harry Reid in the United States, which gave me first-hand insight into politics, policy-making, and the importance of strategic communication. From there, I joined a start-up in San Francisco, immersing myself in the fast-paced, innovative world of entrepreneurship and marketing. I then moved into the finance sector in Vancouver, Canada, gaining valuable commercial and analytical skills. These experiences gave me a diverse perspective and a strong foundation, which I brought with me when I began my legal career in the UK."

What role did mentors and coaches play in your career planning?

"Mentors have played a pivotal role throughout every stage of my career. I've been incredibly fortunate to be surrounded by strong, brilliant women who have not only inspired me but actively shaped my professional journey. From my early days in politics to my time in start-ups, finance, and now law, my mentors have offered guidance, encouragement, and a perspective that has helped me navigate transitions between industries with confidence. They have challenged me to think bigger, refine my skills, and remain resilient in the face of challenges. Having trusted mentors is one of the most valuable assets in any career, and their influence continues to inform the decisions I make today."

Who inspired your career?

"My father was the biggest inspiration for my career. He's a lawyer in the Philippines, and I've always admired how he used his law degree as a foundation to build a successful career in banking and finance. His ability to adapt his legal skills to different industries showed me the versatility and value of a legal education. Watching his career taught me that law is not only a profession but also a powerful platform to explore diverse opportunities and make a real impact."

How did you create time and space to plan your career?

"Creating time and space to plan my career has always been intentional. At key transition points, I've made a conscious effort to step back from day-to-day demands and reflect on what I truly wanted my next chapter to look like. I've found that carving out time – whether through short breaks between roles, structured goal-setting sessions, or simply setting aside quiet moments each week – has been essential for making thoughtful, strategic decisions. This space allowed me to assess my skills, identify gaps, and ensure that each move aligned with my long-term vision, rather than just reacting to immediate opportunities."

What advice would you give to young lawyers at the start of their career about career planning?

"My advice to young lawyers is to see your career as a 'long game' and not to be afraid of taking a less traditional path. Law has always been my chosen career, but I deliberately spent time in other industries before starting my legal practice. Those experiences – in politics, start-ups, and finance – not only broadened my skills but gave me a unique perspective that I now bring to my work as a lawyer. Be curious, say yes to opportunities that push you out of your comfort zone, and seek out mentors who will challenge and support you. Most importantly, carve out regular time to reflect on your goals and check that your current role is moving you towards them. A legal career isn't a straight line, and the detours often end up being the most valuable."

Looking back at your career, what do you wish you had done differently?

"I wish I hadn't compared myself so much to others and had focused more on my own path. Early in my career, I often measured my progress against where my peers were, which sometimes created unnecessary pressure. Over time, I've learned that everyone's journey is different, and success doesn't follow a single timeline. The moments when I trusted my instincts and followed my own direction have been the most rewarding, both professionally and personally."

What are your top three tips to plan your career?

1) Broaden your experience before specializing – this is the only way to figure out what you love to do.
2) Seek out mentors and don't be afraid to put yourself out there.
3) Take time to step back and reflect.

Anything else that you want to add?

"Treat your career like a long game – stay curious, take unexpected opportunities, and make sure every move aligns with your own path, not someone else's."

The role of the physical environment

Using specific spaces and environments can be a useful way to carve out time for quality career planning. Try to find a specific chair, café, room in your home or garden, bench in a public park, or train journey that you associate with quality reflection time and thinking. Head space and time for deep thinking is needed for career planning.

By doing this, you create a positive association called an "anchor" with a specific place for career planning.

Attending a career retreat with a group of others at a similar career crossroads can be very helpful to ring-fence time for career planning. A weekend or week dedicated to your future career strategy and plan is time well spent. I helped out on the Law Society's Returners course for over a decade. The setting of Eynsham Hall in Oxfordshire gave the delegates quality time away from their children and lives to focus on themselves and their careers. In a world interrupted by constant notifications, silence can be golden and highly productive!

Solicitors really lack this with the pressures of the day job, and it is such a good investment of time. Going to a quiet café for half an hour before you go into your office can work very well too. Purposeful focused career planning, little and often, is better than none at all.

The impact of AI on career planning and strategic time management

AI is a useful tool to help solicitors plan their career expediently and thoroughly. For example – when I put the prompt *"What should solicitors be doing in 2025 to plan their careers expediently and thoroughly?"* into an AI model, this is what it gave me:

- Assess achievements and challenges from the past year.
- Set SMART goals.
- Build and upgrade in-demand skills.
- Expand your professional network.
- Consider new and diversifying career paths.
- Stay current on industry trends.
- Invest in lifelong education and qualifications.
- Enhance your personal brand.

The research took ten seconds, included references to dig deeper, and shared a table summarizing the skill domain, why the skill matters, and the skill focus in 2025, plus a checklist. A great quick resource for busy solicitors!

Conclusions

Lawyers lack time and have pressure and full-on workloads that are not always easy to predict. Fee earning targets and having to keep track of how you spend your time can make freeing up time for yourself and career planning a challenge. Making the most of time and not wasting it can be achieved by a combination of methods. These include good prioritization, delegation, using tech tools, being skilled at saying no, avoiding time frittering and not procrastinating, using marginal time such as commuting, time blocking, and setting reminders.

Making time to plan your career is really important. It is easy to postpone, especially with demanding clients, with young children, or at busy times of the year for your legal specialism. The cost of not prioritizing career planning is immense. It may limit your career ambitions, suppress your earnings, make your skills and knowledge obsolete, and thwart your long-term career prospects.

Networks take time to create and build, client relationships to establish and trust to grow, career capital to be evident, further qualifications to save for and study, personal brands to articulate and update. Making time to plan your career will reap rewards and accrue over time.

Career agility is vital in a fast moving and changing world. Making time to plan your career and carve out quality time for deep thinking and strategic time management is a must.

Having read this chapter, block out some time in your diary for action planning.

Career planning self-reflective questions

- How will I deepen and broaden my networks?
- How will I consciously engage my close network?
- How will I create focus and additional energy for an increasingly complex and uncertain world?
- What competencies do I possess that are invaluable/hard for others to copy or machines to replace?
- How will I create differentiation and stand out vs my competitors?
- How will I create/protect time to think about my career strategy?
- How will I build deeper knowledge, insights, and skills?
- What "lost" competencies do I possess that I can rediscover and develop?
- What makes me unique compared with other people who do what I do?
- What is my purpose?
- What is the best way for me to create/develop my own credentials?
- What does success mean to me?
- How will I manage my reputation?
- How will I manage my personal brand?
- What archetypes will I use for my communication strategy?
- What is my career strategy and plan 'A', 'B', and 'C'?
- What do I specialize in?
- What five mastery areas can I develop?
- What are my learning objectives and priorities for continual personal and professional development (CPD) and how will I record these?

- What working life do I want for myself in future?
- What are my career ambitions?
- What is the right work–life balance for me?
- How can pro bono work add to my career capital?
- What work challenges or projects can I actively seek out to support my career strategy?
- What is the opportunity cost to me of not having a career strategy?
- What are my best career assets?
- What are my biggest career risks?
- What's the question I most need to ask myself to carve out time for career planning?

Tips to help you say yes to saying "no"

- Answer this question: *What's the underlying reason why I say yes when I want to say no?*
- Create a clear vision and motivating goals that you really want to achieve. This will help you to say no.
- Know your values – what's important to you. This helps you to say no.
- Aim for a "win–win" not a "win–lose".
- Remember you don't have to over-explain/justify your decision to say no.
- Say no with conviction, not apology.
- If you find email or the telephone easier than face-to-face, use it to say no.
- Offer alternative suggestions and ideas to help out the other person.
- Recall an occasion when you successfully said "no" before dealing with a tricky person/situation.

Self-reflective questions

Reflect on the two questions below to apply to yourself or your own business/firm:

1. What could I put in place this week to help me make time for career planning activities on a regular basis?
2. How could I change my personal habits, business systems, or tech to better prioritize my time for career planning?

References

1   www.lawcareers.net/

2   www.lawsociety.org.uk/career-advice/
3   Brushfield, R, *Career Management for Lawyers. Practical Strategies to Plan Your Next Chapter*: The Law Society, March 2019. https://bookshop.lawsociety.org.uk/p/career-management-for-lawyers-practi-paperback/
4   www.linkedin.com/learning/
5   https://communities.lawsociety.org.uk/sections-home

About Globe Law and Business

Globe Law and Business was established in 2005. From the very beginning, we set out to create legal books that are sufficiently high level to be of real use to the experienced professional, yet still accessible and easy to navigate. Most of our authors are drawn from Magic Circle and other top commercial firms, both in the United Kingdom and internationally.
Our titles are carefully produced, with the utmost attention paid to editorial, design and production processes. We hope this results in high-quality publications that are easy to read and a pleasure to own.

In 2021, we were very pleased to announce the start of a new chapter for Globe Law and Business following the acquisition of law books under the imprint Ark Publishing. Our law firm management list is now significantly expanded with many well-known and loved Ark Publishing titles.

We are also pleased to announce the launch of our online content platform, Globe Law Online, which allows for easy access across firms. Details of all titles included can be found at www.globelawonline.com. Email glo@globelawandbusiness.com for further details and to arrange a free trial for you or your firm.

We'd very much like to hear from you with your thoughts and ideas for improving what we offer. Please do feel free to email me on sian@globelawandbusiness.com. Happy reading and thank you for your time.

Sian O'Neill
Managing director
Globe Law and Business
www.globelawandbusiness.com

www.ingramcontent.com/pod-product-compliance
Ingram Content Group UK Ltd.
Pitfield, Milton Keynes, MK11 3LW, UK
UKHW020043061025
463588UK00001BA/4